Caring
for Widows

For Pastor & Mrs. Howe,

Faithful servants who
love the Lord & His people.
Caring for Widows
Wes Teterud

James 1:27

Caring
for Widows

You and Your Church
Can Make a Difference

WESLEY M. TETERUD

FOREWORD BY JOHN F. MACARTHUR JR.

Baker Books

A Division of Baker Book House Co
Grand Rapids, Michigan 49516

© 1994 by Wesley M. Teterud

Published by Baker Books
a division of Baker Book House Company
P.O. Box 6287, Grand Rapids, Michigan 49516-6287

Printed in the United States of America

Library of Congress Cataloging-in-Publication Data

Teterud, Wesley M.
    Caring for widows : you and your church can make a
      difference / Wesley M. Teterud ; foreword by John F.
      MacArthur Jr.
        p.   cm.
    Includes bibliographical references.
    ISBN 0-8010-8909-3
    1. Church work with widows.   I. Title
    BV4445.T47   1994
    254′.08′654—dc20   93-1763

Scripture quotations not otherwise identified are from the HOLY BIBLE, NEW INTERNATIONAL VERSION®. NIV®. Copyright © 1973, 1978, 1984 by International Bible Society. Used by permission of Zondervan Publishing House. All rights reserved. Other references are from the King James Version (KJV) and New King James Version (NKJV).

CONTENTS ॐ

Appendices

ACKNOWLEDGMENTS

No NOVICE AUTHOR makes a literary contribution without standing on the shoulders of others, having veteran authors blaze the trail for him, or receiving support from both family and friends. The following names are those who helped me launch my first book. I am deeply grateful.

To Carl Laney and Robert Anderson, professors at Western Conservative Baptist Seminary, who read my manuscript and encouraged me to disseminate its contents through print. To Richard Mayhue, vice president of The Master's Seminary, who graciously interacted with this work and went to bat for me on this project in a number of significant ways.

To Earl Radmacher, president emeritus of Phoenix Western Seminary; John Davis, president of Grace Theological Seminary; and Homer Kent, Jr., professor emeritus of Grace Theological Seminary, who all wrote endorsement letters in my behalf to get this book published.

To John MacArthur, Jr., pastor at Grace Community Church and president of The Master's College and Seminary, for his willingness to write the foreword.

To Jane Goenner, who worked with me on editing the original manuscript. To the leaders and faithful members of the Emmanuel Bible Church who allowed me the freedom to implement many of the ideas of this book in our own ministry. To my secretary, Carol Little, who served as a continual help in guarding my schedule and performing countless tasks for a pastor who is writing a book.

To Paul Engle, editor at Baker Book House, for his encouragement and clear communication to me at every step of the publication process. To my good friend Ed Mattfeld, who assisted me with all of my computer needs to do the actual writing of the book. To all of the widows in the Widow's Might Ministry who model the principles and suggestions found in this book.

To attorney Bjarne Johnson, Jr., insurance agent Frank Witt, Jr., investment advisor Phil Thoeny, and pastor Mike Wing, who gave me professional assistance in their fields of expertise.

Finally, to my parents, Morris and Dorothy Teterud, who developed in me a sensitivity toward the care for widows at an early age. To my wife, Sunny, and my children, Matt, Tim, and Sarah, who gave me the family support necessary to complete this book.

FOREWORD   🙠

NEVER HAVE I encountered such a thorough, biblical presentation of the vital matter of God's compassion for widows that carries through to the practical plan which can be reproduced for everyday life in the church. Wes Teterud contributes a delightful discussion with *Caring for Widows: You and Your Church Can Make a Difference.* He offers even more in the book than the title promises.

I'm reminded that Christ looked with compassion on the multitudes because they were like sheep without a shepherd (Matt. 9:36). Compassion reflects Christ's heart. Thus his body, the church, should always be poised to respond on his behalf with compassion for those in need.

Jesus granted sight to the blind (Matt. 20:34), cleansed lepers (Mark 1:41), fed the hungry crowd (Matt. 15:32), and raised the dead (Luke 7:12–13) all because he had compassion for them. This prominent feature in God's character also stands "center stage" in much of our Lord's teaching—most memorably in the Good Samaritan (Luke 10:33) and the Prodigal Son (Luke 15:20). Since compassion fueled Christ's actions and exhortations, certainly the church should be so impelled.

For years Grace Community Church has taken a special interest in its widows because our elders have taken the Scriptures seriously. We have visited and revisited Acts 6:1–6, 1 Timothy 5:3–16, and other key biblical instructions only to be convinced of God's high priority in caring for such godly women who look to the Lord as their help in time of trouble. Even though our ministry to widows has emerged in various forms over many seasons, our sense of responsibility has always been to live out the timeless truth that "this is pure and undefiled religion in the sight of our God and Father, to visit orphans and widows in their distress" (James 1:27).

Dr. Teterud writes not as an armchair theorist but as one who labored hard to forge out of the impeccable, raw materials of Scripture an eminently usable ministry pattern for the local church. These studies and plans for ministry gush out of a deep, authentic well. He noticeably contributes from the overflow of his own growing passion to be like Christ.

We will be using this volume as a resource at Grace Community Church and in The Master's Seminary classroom. I enthusiastically commend *Caring for Widows* as required reading for learning to mirror Christ's compassion before our own generation.

John F. MacArthur Jr.

INTRODUCTION ❧

THE TELEPHONE rang at 6:00 A.M., and the terrified voice at the other end cried out, "Pastor! Something has happened to Vern!"

The startling news woke me out of a deep sleep as if I had been hit by a bucket of cold water. "Where are you, Susan?" I asked.

"I'm on my way to the hospital now," she replied.

"I'll meet you there," I assured her.

Vern and Susan were thirtysomething, happily married, employed in full-time ministry at our church, and the recent parents of an adopted baby girl. A few years earlier, surgeons had removed a tumor on Vern's pituitary gland. But a new tumor developed, and Vern required another delicate brain surgery. This time complications set in during recovery, and Susan joined the ranks of the 500,000 American wives widowed each year.[1]

Susan represents the more than eight out of ten wives who are widowed in their lifetime.[2] Susan's bleak prospect of spending an average eighteen years as a widow was moderated by her young age.[3] But her immediate thoughts after her significant loss were certainly not on remarriage.

Several misconceptions about widowhood are held by both family members and friends of widows. Many perceive widowhood as only a geriatric problem. Others assume that most widows will remarry. Some believe that most widows are left with adequate life insurance, that they recover from grief in a few months, and that they will ask for help when they need it. These misconceptions must be erased for the concerned to effectively care for widows.

Widows like Susan belong to local churches and form one of the most neglected segments of the church community. Generalizations about widows and insensitivities toward them in the Christian community have led to inappropriate care and, in some cases, a total failure to care for the needs of the widows in the churches. However, some churches are doing a fine job of caring for widows and making such care a top priority in their ministries.

The purpose of this book is to awaken the conscience of the body of Christ to the needs of widows and to equip Christians to fulfill the biblical mission to "visit the widow in her affliction" (James 1:27). The church of Jesus Christ must return to the priority of caring for widows like Susan.

Just as the early church mobilized during the crisis that resulted from the neglect of the daily care of widows' needs (Acts 6:1–6), so the contemporary church must once again renew its commitment to the care of widows. This commitment is even more urgent when we see the threat of government programs such as Social Security being cut, the megapopulation of baby boomers rapidly approaching the median age of widowhood (fifty-six years of age), and the fact that 85 percent of all married women will eventually be widowed.[4]

This book targets several types of readers: those who are engaged as professional care givers (pastors, counselors, chaplains, funeral directors, physicians, nurses), church leaders (elders, deacons, deaconesses), and other laypersons serving in local churches. Family members and, of course, widows themselves will also benefit from reading this book.

My intention is not to burden pastors by adding another responsibility (care for widows) to the tremendous work loads they already carry in their local church ministries. Hopefully, this book will ease a pastor's load by providing him with a tool to share with widows, family members, and friends of widows who often look to him for guidance. It is not the pastor's job alone to care for the widows in the church. In fact, the Bible exhorts family members to care for their own widows so that the church will not be burdened to look after their welfare (1 Tim. 5:4, 8, 16). The people who usually have the most contact with widows and have the best understanding of their specific needs can, in turn, implement the ideas from this book and draw from these resources to care for the needs of the widows.

The background material for this book originates from volumes of research, hours of personal interviews with widows, years of practical involvement as a pastor in the lives of widows, and the organization and operation of a ministry to widows at the Emmanuel Bible Church.

The term *widow* used throughout this book refers to a woman who has lost her husband by physical death. Divorced women, those abandoned by their husbands, and those living with disabled husbands certainly have many of the same needs as widows (financial, emotional, spiritual). However, there are also many differences between these women and widows. The focus of this book will be on the unique plight of widows.

Several observations in my years of ministry have directed my focus to particular issues related to widowhood. I have found that society as a whole, and the church specifically, are generally offering inadequate support to widows, although I am thankful for the notable exceptions. I have also discovered that society and the church often neglect widows because of a lack of concern for them. One of my colleagues in ministry advised me to consider a broader topic which would not be restricted to widows, because he doubted whether people are that concerned about taking care of them.

One of the significant reasons we should give priority to the care of widows is that God makes it a high priority for Christians. Both the Old and New Testaments embraced and championed the cause of widows (see appendix F). Churches must give more attention to the care of widows because the Bible instructs them to care for them.

Many care givers, church leaders, family members, and widows are either not aware of or are confused about their roles as they relate to widowhood. Many professional care givers have told me that they feel ill-equipped to assist widows in grief. I have heard widows commonly complain that family members and friends tend to forget them shortly after the funeral. I have also observed that church people may grow insensitive to the long-term needs of widows and unintentionally neglect them. A concern to care for widows, however, can be aroused within these significant members of the widow's "new" family.

If Christians desire to please the Lord, and they see from the Scriptures that caring for widows is one way to accomplish this desire, then people can learn how to carry out this biblical responsibility. The intent of this book is to show how you and your church can make a difference by caring in practical ways for widows.

1 God's Special Care

੩▲

IMAGINE THAT YOU are the king or queen of an early civilization in the ancient Near East. You have come to the end of your reign and you want to be remembered as a successful ruler. What would you like the epitaph on your tomb to read?

The success of a king in ancient Near Eastern societies was often judged by how well he took care of the widows in his kingdom. When a country began to experience social and moral decay, this deterioration was often reflected in the demise of the protection of widows. Widows were sold as credit-slaves and kept in a state of slavery for a lifetime during such social declines of a country. "To obliterate this abuse, laws and also religious pressure were used as compulsory methods to protect the rights of this group."[1]

Ancient literature provides strong support for the high priority given to the protection of and provision for widows in their plight. The most impressive body of literature addressing the needs of widows is found in the Bible.

Both the Old and New Testaments are abundant with references to the plight of widowhood. Because of the unique condition of widows, God personally assumes responsibility in the care of widows:

> For the LORD your God is God of gods and Lord of lords, the great God, mighty and awesome, who shows no par-

1

tiality and accepts no bribes. He defends the cause of the fatherless and the widow, and loves the alien, giving him food and clothing (Deut. 10:17–18).

The Psalms tell us that God is the only one who can give justice and deliverance to widows in their plight. In Psalm 68:5 God is called "a defender of widows," and Psalm 146:9 says that God "sustains the fatherless and widow." In three areas God's special care for widows is evident throughout the Bible.

Protecting Widows

Widowhood places women in an extremely vulnerable position. This was especially true in biblical times when a Jewish wife did not inherit her husband's possessions. In Israel, the oldest male child was recognized as the head of each family after his father died. The widow under this economy was left with only the possessions she had brought into the marriage: her personal dowry and marriage gifts.

Tamar, the first widow recorded in the Old Testament (Gen. 38), is seen as one who is dependent on the male members of her former husband's family, because she did not have a son to receive her husband's inheritance. The story ends on a tragic note when she conceives twins by her father-in-law in a desperate attempt to have her own child as an heir.

Since widows were left unprotected in their plight of inheritance, two great needs arose. The first need was protection against exploitation of what they possessed through their oldest sons, and the second was the need for adequate living provisions in their time of distress.

Savings and Loans

God provided protection for widows in Israel by establishing laws related to their financial dilemma. One of these laws is found in Deuteronomy 24:17: "Do not deprive the alien or the fatherless of justice, or take the cloak of the widow as a pledge."

The garment spoken of in the text was a blanketlike piece of clothing used as a cloak during the day and as a bed covering at night. A poor widow would only have her garment to offer as a pledge for collateral to secure a loan. The lender was commanded not to insist upon the widow's only personal protection against the elements by day and night as collateral.[2]

Proverbs 15:25 states that God "keeps the widow's boundaries intact." This is yet another way in which God protected the financial interests of widows in biblical times. From the beginning of Israel's conquest of the Promised Land under the capable leadership of Joshua, God divided this land among every tribe and family of Israel.

Once the land was allocated, a crude survey of the inheritance was marked by either a heap of stones, a natural feature (river, tree, etc.), or a double furrow of plowed land. Once the landmarks were in place (Prov. 15:25), they could never be moved, because to do so was to alter the gift of God (Deut. 19:14).

Land to a widow in those days was tantamount to a life insurance policy left to a widow today. Although a Hebrew wife did not directly inherit the land from her husband, she nevertheless enjoyed the financial security of her son's possession of the land. How would a widow's land be protected if she did not have a male member to secure it from creditors?

Preventing Chapter Eleven

A widow could lose her property if her husband had incurred substantial debt. If she had no son to inherit it, her property could revert to her husband's family. She would be destitute. She would lose her only means of livelihood. To prevent a widow from being forced to file "chapter eleven" (bankruptcy), God established the institution of *go'el*.

The word *go'el* comes from a root word in the Hebrew language which means "to buy back or to redeem" or "to lay claim to," but fundamentally it meant "to protect." Leviticus 25:25 explains this institution: "If one of your countrymen becomes poor and sells some of his property, his nearest relative is to come and redeem what his countryman has sold."

"The *go'el* was a redeemer, a protector, a defender of the interests of the group."[3] This legal provision to secure a widow's land estate through the process of *go'el* is clearly illustrated in the biblical story of Ruth. Boaz became the *go'el* of Naomi and Ruth by purchasing the family property which was in jeopardy of being sold outside of the family (Ruth 4:9–10).

God demonstrated special care for widows by protecting them in their economic plight. His special care is further demonstrated by the provisions specifically issued to widows.

Providing for Widows

Today, destitute widows qualify for assistance from the government in the form of welfare benefits, food stamps, and medical assistance. Impoverished widows during biblical times did not enjoy the same provisions as those of their contemporary counterparts. Though they had many needs, food was one of the most immediate needs of widows in ancient times.

Daily Bread

There were two ways in which the food needs for widows were confronted in Israel. Deuteronomy 14:28–29 and 26:12–13 describe the food bank that was established by the tithes of the people. The legislation of the Old Testament required the Israelite community as a whole to tithe a portion of their income and produce to a central food bank located at the nearest town.

This program was comparable to our current government surplus programs, which issue commodities such as milk, cheese, and eggs to those in our society who experience food shortages. This tithe occurred every three years after harvest. During the intervals between the storing of the tithes of the third year, the widows had another option available—gleaning.

The gleaning laws contained in Deuteronomy 24:17–22 required property owners to purposely leave generous portions of sheaves on the ground, olives on the trees, and grapes on the vines after harvest for the widows to glean. Significantly, the preservation of the widow's integrity was linked to the process of gleaning. Rather than beg or seek a handout, widows would go into the fields and orchards after the harvest and, like the farmer, work for their own food by gleaning the leftovers.

Typically, a woman's husband is her breadwinner. When she loses her husband through death, she loses a significant amount of financial support. Today a wife's income level drops on the average of 44 percent after her husband dies.[4] God provided for Old Testament widows in another special way by a unique system of remarriage.

A New Husband

Remember, a Hebrew widow did not inherit her husband's estate. The land was inherited by her oldest son. But what happened if a widow was childless? What would happen to her husband's land? How would a widow in this case be supported? God provided the opportunity for a widow to remarry her eligible brother-in-law, which would assure her of carrying on the family name and securing the family estate.

This opportunity is found in the Old Testament practice of levirate marriage. Levirate refers to a brother-in-law, and the law for levirate marriage is given in Deuteronomy 25:5–10.

According to the levirate law, if brothers lived together and one of them died without offspring, one of the surviving brothers took his widow as a wife, and the first-born son of this new union was regarded by law as the heir to the deceased's estate. The custom of levirate marriage assimilated the widow into the family of her husband, which would afford her the privileges and benefits that she and her former husband had worked for prior to his death.

It was not easy for a brother-in-law to refuse to marry the widow. If he did refuse such an obligation, the widow took him before the legal authorities of Israel and filed formal charges against her brother-in-law (Deut. 25:7). Once the brother-in-law declared that he did not want to marry his widowed sister-in-law, a ceremony of humiliation was conducted. The widow removed his sandal from his foot (indicating that the brother had abandoned his responsibility), she spat in his face, and recited, "This is what is done to the man who will not build up his brother's family line" (Deut. 25:9). The levirate law was drafted by God to demonstrate his loving concern for widows and their families.

Justice

It can be extremely easy to take advantage of widows in their condition. Since they have lost their providers and protectors (husbands), some widows are vulnerable to swindlers, gimmicks, and other negative influences designed to take advantage of them. It was no different in biblical times.

Job 24 portrays evil ones as those who oppressed widows. For this reason, Job's companions speculated that his suffering was for the possible violation of having afflicted widows. Isaiah began the chorus of prophetic voices by serving notice to the sinful nation of Israel to repent and treat widows fairly (Isa. 1:17). The sin of neglecting widows in the land had permeated the highest levels of government (Isa. 1:23; 9:16–17; 10:1–2).

The weeping prophet, Jeremiah, proclaimed a stinging rebuke to Judah for acting unfairly toward the fatherless and widows (Jer. 5:28). The kings of Judah were admonished to act in justice and in fairness toward those who could not defend themselves against the oppressor (Jer. 22:3). Jeremiah's lament was that "our mothers are like widows" (Lam. 5:3).

Ezekiel joins the chorus of prophetic voices against the abuse shown toward widows (Ezek. 22:7), and Malachi completes the prophetic denunciation against the unfair treatment of widows. Malachi lists the exploitation of widows right along with the sins of sorcery, adultery, and perjury (Mal. 3:5). God's special care for widows is seen in both his protection and provisions on their behalf. One other area displays God's special care for widows.

Priority in the Church

The church is described in the New Testament as a body, which implies that it is characterized as both an organization and a living organism. The church consists of all genuine born-again believers. Jesus predicted its birth in Matthew 16:18, where he stated that he was the owner, builder, and maintainer of the church. Colossians 1:18 tells us that Christ is the "head of the body, the church." This means that the members of the body (Christians) are to receive directions from the head and follow these directions. What is Jesus' view about widows?

Learning from the Head

We can investigate three areas of the life of our Lord to determine his level of concern for widows. The first area consists of his personal life when he was here on earth.

Widows in Jesus' Life

Widows bracketed Jesus' life. He was met shortly after his birth by an eighty-four-year-old widow named Anna (Luke 2:36–38). His exit of the world was marked by the presence of another widow, his own mother, Mary.

John 19:26–27 is the account of Jesus entrusting his widowed mother to the care of his dear friend, John. The words spoken here by Jesus were some of his last words as he hung on the cross. One writer states, "In these last words of Jesus upon the cross, He laid open His inmost soul, and in them He exemplified the spiritual principles He had been teaching."[5]

Jesus showed by his own example that there is no excuse for neglecting widows. Entrusting his mother to John's care was one of his last acts on earth. Even on the cross, Jesus was not unmindful of his duty to care for his widowed mother.

Widows in Jesus' Ministry

Another area in which Jesus manifested special care for widows was in his earthly ministry. This is especially seen when Jesus met a funeral procession one day during his ministry (Luke 7:11–17).

The funeral was in honor of a boy whose grieving mother was a widow. Jesus, who was moved with compassion, chose to raise the dead boy back to life. The divine miracle to bring the widow's son back to life may have removed any practical threats of the widow becoming destitute, since she had lost all of her male support.

The religious lawyers (scribes) of Jesus' day took advantage of widows by extracting money from them in unscrupulous ways. They added to their own finances by exploiting the household assets of widows. Jesus warned these religious charlatans against the heinous sins of "devouring" widows' houses (Matt. 23:14; Mark 12:40; Luke 20:47).

Widows did not go unnoticed in the everyday life of our Lord. He observed their plight and championed their defense. One final area supports Jesus' care for widows.

Widows in Jesus' Teaching

On three separate occasions Jesus used widows as object lessons to teach spiritual truths. His use of widows as illustrations in his teaching provided a symbol of vulnerability, weakness, and spiritual sensitivity.

The first example of Jesus using a widow to communicate a spiritual lesson is found in Luke 4:25–26. Jesus referred to the Old Testament widow of Zarephath who believed Elijah's word of prophecy. The second example is found in Luke 18:1–8, where Jesus spoke a parable about a widow who desperately sought justice from a conscienceless judge. The third example is found in Jesus' teaching about the widow's mites (Mark 12:41–44).

Jesus knew about the social problems facing the widows of his day, and he was not afraid to speak out against the injustices widows experienced. He cared about the widow to the same degree that his Father cared in Old Testament times. The high place that widows held in the life of Jesus explains why he gave additional instructions on the care for widows to the church in the Epistles (1 Cor. 7:8; 1 Tim. 5:3–16; James 1:27).

Learning from Body Life

Imagine that you are an apostle at the time the church began at Pentecost. Your church is experiencing the kind of growth that would cause church-growth experts to investigate your success. You have seen amazing acts of God's power through the conversions of thousands of Jews and Gentiles, miraculous healings, and tremendous opportunities to evangelize throughout your city and the surrounding regions. Definite church discipline was witnessed by you and the others in the local body as Ananias and Sapphira dropped dead as a result of lying about their offerings. Your witness has caused the city fathers to call emergency city-council meetings to deal with the great spiritual sensation which is having an impact on everyone in the area.

You have been involved in your own share of meetings with the other apostles. The men have been studying the Old Testament prophecies in light of the recent crucifixion and resurrection of Jesus. Prayer for the church and community are offered at each apostles' meeting. The meetings seem to extend longer into the evenings as the church continues to grow.

One evening you hear a knock on the door. It is one of the Greek-speaking Jewish widows, who is the spokeswoman for the other widows of her ethnic group. She is at your home to register a complaint. She and the other widows feel they are being overlooked in the daily distribution of food from the church's benevolent pantry. They have noticed there is always enough food for the Hebrew-speaking widows, but when it comes time for these widows to receive their portion of food, there is a shortage. The widow asks you to discuss the problem with the other apostles at your next meeting.

It was this type of problem which forced the early church to organize for the purpose of taking care of the widows (Acts 6:1–7). The apostles did not want to abandon their priority of prayer and preaching, but neither did they want to neglect the care of widows in the church. The first item on their agenda was to organize in such a way that both priorities would be accomplished.

One of the immediate lessons to emerge from life in the early church was its natural response to the care of widows. This responsibility was not relegated to the social programs of the government. It was a natural, normal development from the Jewish background of the first Christians.

It is apparent that the leaders of the first church were

sensitive enough to the problem of caring for widows that they organized in an effective way. Once the church mobilized to care for these widows, the results that followed were positive (Acts 6:7). There seems to be a close relationship between God's blessing upon the church and the church's proper response to the plight of widows. This correlation extends from the Old Testament teachings where God's blessing either resided on those who would or was withdrawn from those who would not care for widows (Exod. 22:22–24; Deut. 24:19).

Acts 9:36–43 provides another glimpse into the body life of the early church. Dorcas (Tabitha) was a woman characterized as "always doing good and helping the poor" (Acts 9:36). A significant number of widows were mourning her death as they stood by the apostle Peter and showed him the various garments and clothing which Dorcas had made for them (v. 39).

Dorcas represented a model Christian who sacrificially gave of herself to assist widows in their plight. Peter chose to exercise his apostolic authority by raising her from the dead. Stahlin concludes that "the raising of Tabitha thus took place in the interest of widows like the raisings at Zarephath and Nain."[6]

The example of Dorcas as it relates to her interest in widows illustrates again the accompanying blessings extended to those who care about widows. In her case, it meant the blessing of the rare miracle to be brought back from the dead.

Summary

In answering the question, Who cares about the widow? it is evident from the Scriptures that God certainly cares. No other minority group receives the same degree of attention from the Lord as that of widows. This special class of women is promised that God himself will be their defender.

Three foundational concepts appear in God's special care for widows. The first concept is preparation for widowhood. God prepared to meet the needs of widows by legislating laws in their favor, introducing institutions that would assist them, and blessing nations who would honor widows in the land. The second concept is God's protection for widows. The third concept is God's provision for widows. The Lord feeds, clothes, and houses widows who are destitute. He works through his people to provide for the needs of widows.

These three concepts form the basis for any ministry to widows. They are timeless concepts that affect widows of any era. There will always be a need to prepare people to care for widows. There will also be a continuing need to protect widows from dangers inherent in their distress as well as the need to provide for their material shortages in their affliction. Plans for all of these will have to be made if the church takes seriously the exhortation "to look after widows in their distress" (James 1:27).

Questions for Discussion

1. Why does the Bible seem to give so much attention to the care of widows specifically? Why are widowers or divorced people not given the same emphasis in Scripture?

2. Why should the Christian care about the widow, according to scriptural teachings? Is there a relationship between the church's care for widows today and attendant blessings from God?

3. Why have some churches neglected the biblical responsibility to care for widows? What are some of the social influences effecting such neglect? What are some of the spiritual influences effecting such neglect?

4. How can your church begin to minister to widows in practical ways of preparation, protection, and provision for them?

Application

1. Conduct a survey of the widows in your church and have them list the five most common fears they face as widows.

2. Assign a deacon and/or elder husband-and-wife team to visit at least one widow in your church to gather a specific list of needs each widow has that she can neither afford nor fulfill herself.

3. Schedule to discuss the plight of widows in your church at one of your board meetings. You may consider inviting the widows from the church to sit in on the meeting to offer suggestions.

4. Arrange for a Sunday school class or a series of sermons on the church's responsibility to care for widows.

2 A Rainbow of Widows

❧

"I JUST REALIZED that my daughter is a widow," Susan's father told a group of men who were assembled in my office. "My perception of widows comes from our senior-saints Sunday school class where the widows are gray-haired, elderly women. It has just hit me that my young daughter is now a widow!"

Susan's father expressed what most of us assume about widowhood. We do not fully understand the types of widows represented in our churches. We look at the elderly widows in our congregations and view them as if they have always been widowed and old. I held this misconception about one widow in our church whom I had known before I ever became her pastor. I learned that she had been widowed twice. She was widowed the first time when she was in her twenties and had a young child.

Widows come in a variety of ages, from different backgrounds, and have experienced individual and distinct losses. The individuality of a widow must not be usurped by a stereotype. Each widow possesses a unique personality which requires individual consideration.

Although each widow is unique, the Bible mentions some general categories of widows to help us understand certain universal characteristics of widowhood. These categories are given in the classic New Testament passage concerning widows.

First Timothy gives more attention to the church's care for widows than to any other important subject. The fourteen verses of 1 Timothy 5:3–16 occupy greater space than that given to public prayer (2:1–8), the role of women in public worship (2:9–15), the qualifications for elders (3:1–7), the qualifications for deacons (3:8–13), the description of false teachers (4:1–5), and the exhortation to the rich (6:17–19).

Homer Kent, Jr., arranges the material in this passage on widows in a topical grouping of five different categories. Paul distinguishes several kinds of widows in 1 Timothy 5, but these five groups are not completely independent of each other. Each group calls for special treatment.[1]

"Real" Widows

Paul begins his discourse on caring for widows by stating: "Give proper recognition to those widows who are really in need" (1 Tim. 5:3). The New King James Version calls them "widows who are really widows." What constitutes a "real" widow? Does this imply that there are fake widows running around?

Martha was a young Vietnamese lady who came to America as a refugee from the Vietnam War. Her husband, an American businessman, was killed during the war, necessitating her evacuation and that of her son from Vietnam. She and her infant son arrived in the United States separated from her family, friends, and culture. Providentially, the Lord led Martha and her son to an Air Force base in Montana for relocation and settlement purposes. Eventually, Martha came to Great Falls, Montana, became a Christian, and joined the Emmanuel Bible Church.

Since Martha was a new widow in the church, and she had a language barrier, the people of Emmanuel did not fully understand that she was destitute. We knew she was receiving government assistance, but we did not realize that this aid was insufficient to meet her needs.

Her status as a real widow was driven home to our congregation when we discovered she was forced to make a meal from a dead bird lodged in the grill of her automobile. On another occasion, her menu consisted of meat from a rabbit that had been struck by a vehicle on the road. When the members of Emmanuel Bible Church learned that Martha's diet was dependent on roadkill, we finally woke up and began to monitor her welfare.

The real widow is one who lacks any kind of family or financial support. Martha definitely fit this description. She was separated from her family by thousands of miles, she had no marketable skills for work in the United States, and her health was not good. Hundreds of widows in America survive by eating food from the dumpsters of fast-food restaurants. Many widows live among the homeless of our land. They are destitute.

Verse 5 describes this type of widow in the church by saying that she is "left all alone, puts her hope in God and continues night and day to pray and to ask God for help." The real widow cannot necessarily count on remarriage as an option for support. The church is primarily responsible to provide regular assistance for this type of widow (vv. 3, 16).

Widows with Family

Contrasted with the real widow is the widow who is not completely alone (1 Tim. 5:4, 8, 16). Bridgette's situation illustrates this second category.

Bridgette called after midnight to inform me that she received word her husband had been killed. Randy was making his last run with a semi-trailer before entering a new career in the real estate business when he wrecked the truck and was dead at the scene of the accident.

My wife and I immediately went to Bridgette's home to spend the remainder of the early morning hours with her until family members from Colorado began to arrive. Bridgette and her young daughter were soon surrounded by caring family members. Eventually Bridgette moved from Montana to Colorado to be with her family.

This second category of widows includes those who are not left totally alone with no potential financial support. Family members of widows are instructed in 1 Timothy 5:4 to care for their own. In fact, verse 8 issues a serious statement to families about taking care of their widows: "If anyone does not provide for his relatives, and especially for his immediate family, he has denied the faith and is worse than an unbeliever."

Sometimes this passage is used out of context to teach against slothfulness and for the importance of providing a living for one's family. The thrust of the teaching, however, is directed to family members of widows who need to provide for them. If family members shirk their responsibility in caring for their own widows, the Bible states, they have "denied the faith and [are] worse than an unbeliever."

One of my former seminary professors took this passage of Scripture seriously by establishing a savings account for his widowed mother, into which his brothers and sisters could make systematic deposits to her account to meet her financial needs. In larger families where there are four or more children, a monthly contribution of ten dollars per month by each child to an interest-bearing account accumulates quickly.

I adopted the practice of meeting with the male members of a new widow's family after the meal which is usually provided for family and friends at the church following the funeral service. My purpose for meeting with these men is to show them their biblical responsibility to protect and provide for their newly inherited widow. Normally, I include only the Christian male members of the widow's family in this meeting, but there are times when a non-Christian will attend. Only believers can fully appreciate what God's Word says on the matter of filial responsibility in caring for widows.

Widows Who Like to Party

The hedonistic (pleasure-seeking) widow is addressed in 1 Timothy 5:6. The description of this particular woman, "living for [sensual] pleasure," is taken from a Greek word that refers to sheep who are living in a rich green pasture, which makes them frisky. The point of this term is that her main purpose is to party and make a good catch of a man.

I am familiar with one widow who frequented the bars and dated non-Christian men after her husband's death. A seventy-year-old woman, she attempted to fashion herself like a teenager. She was flirtatious and silly with most men she met. This individual dropped out of church and lived only for the pleasures of this world. Verse 6 tells us that this type of widow is spiritually dead, even though she is physically alive. Some Bible scholars conclude that Paul does not allude to the woman in this category as a "widow" because she is undeserving of the title.

Widows Who Qualify for Senior Discounts

Some difficulties arise when the fourth group of widows is considered (1 Tim. 5:9–10). Some see a definite class of widows established in this group.[2] Others deny the establishment of any special class and consider these two verses simply to refer to the consideration of the special needs of older widows.[3]

It appears that some kind of an official list of widows was intended, since there is also an accompanying set of qualifications required for them to be included. It is not unreasonable to conclude that enrolled widows consisted of real widows (1 Tim. 5:3) who relied on the church for regular support. The remainder of this composition of enrolled widows may have been those who were victims of family neglect (1 Tim. 5:8).

The widows had to be at least sixty years old to qualify for this special list. This does not mean that the church would deprive younger widows of support (1 Tim. 5:3, 5). Younger widows have a better chance of remarrying, and their health is generally better than the older widow's, which may explain why they were excluded from this list.

Younger Widows

I have stated before that widowhood is not a geriatric problem. One out of four widows in the United States is under the age of forty-five.[4] This translates into three million widows who are in their late teens, twenties, thirties, and early forties.[5] An army!

This final category of widows in 1 Timothy 5 is addressed in verses 11–15 (the largest treatment of all the categories in this passage). These women appear to be some of the most spiritually vulnerable widows. The in-

structions warn the church about accepting or support-
ing younger widows who stray from the Lord in their
widowhood.

The pitfalls of idleness, gossip, and meddling mark the
spiritually wayward widow. Young widows are encouraged to remarry and maintain a domestic lifestyle so as
to give no room for the enemy of the gospel to talk
negatively.

Summary

There are as many different types of widows as colors
in the rainbow, and their personalities are as unique as
snowflakes. Although they have many things in common such as loneliness, grief, and worry, each widow is
different in many respects.

This information is critical for the church to understand to effectively minister to widows. Widows must not
be grouped into one large category with resulting erroneous assumptions about their needs. The instructions in
1 Timothy 5 regarding widows provide the church a
general understanding of some of the situations widows
may experience. These instructions must be passed on to
family members of widows, to church leaders who must
be sure real widows are not neglected within the fellowship, and to widows themselves who need to be warned
of the pitfalls of widowhood (especially those related to
younger widows).

Questions for Discussion

1. How does an understanding of the different categories of widows found in 1 Timothy 5:3–16 assist in de-

veloping more effective care for widows in the local church?

2. What are some practical ways Christians could assist the "real" widow? The widow with family? The pleasure-seeking widow? The older widow? The younger widow?

3. Could 1 Timothy 5:8 ("providing for his own") apply to a husband providing adequate life insurance for his wife? Why or why not?

4. What seems to be the significance of the special widows' roll in 1 Timothy 5:9–10? Is it an official roll? What is the purpose of such a roll?

5. Why does Paul desire to see younger widows re-marry (v. 14)?

6. What are some practical ways family members could prepare to assist their widows and relieve the church?

Application

1. List the widows who are in your circle of influence (family, church, community, etc.). Identify the categories each of these widows may fit into generally from 1 Timothy 5:3–16.

2. Identify any "real" widows in your fellowship who lack both family and financial support. Research practical ways you and your church can assist these widows on a regular basis.

3. Provide an opportunity to sit down with family members of widows to teach the principles of 1 Timothy 5:3–16. Develop a system of feedback to hold these members accountable for their responsibility in caring for their widows.

4. Interview both an older widow and a younger widow to determine some of the similarities and differences in their needs.

3 Visiting Widows

৯

Susan HAD PRODUCED stuffed animals to generate extra income while Vern was alive. Her business grew rapidly, and at the time of Vern's death she was overwhelmed by the demands of her business. To add to her pressures, Susan's toddler daughter controlled much of her time.

Jeannie, a woman in our church who had four children of her own, faithfully went to Susan's home on several evenings to assist her in sewing, caring for the toddler, or just to visit to help Susan pass the lonely evenings without her spouse.

Susan appreciated Jeannie's efforts, for, as she stated, "I miss having an adult to talk with at the end of the day. When I am with a two-year-old all day, my visiting is rather confined."

James 1:27 reads: "Religion that God our Father accepts as pure and faultless is this: to look after orphans and widows in their distress and to keep oneself from being polluted by the world." The King James Version says "to visit . . . widows in their affliction."

What does it mean to visit widows? What type of a visit makes such an activity pure and faultless religion before God?

A Social Call?

The term James used for "visit" spoke of the activities of a king who would carry out an inspection or investigation. The idea behind this term was a person's concern about a widow and sense of responsibility for her welfare. To visit widows in their trouble is more than merely to make social calls, although it may begin here.

To visit widows in the New Testament sense of the word means to become involved in their lives and to aid them in practical ways. Visiting widows requires a continual monitoring of their needs (financial, emotional, spiritual, home repairs, etc.). Calling on widows necessitates sensitivity to what they are experiencing (fears, frustrations, accomplishments, etc.).

The typical problem in visiting widows is that the practice becomes short-lived. A widow receives many visitors before, during, and shortly after her husband's death. But after the funeral visitors drop off as if the widow has the plague. The widow's life is radically altered, but her friends and family resume their lives. A callousness develops with many of these close associates of a widow, and the kind of visiting required at this time in her life decreases significantly. Widows frequently report that they feel many of their family and friends withdraw from them shortly after their husbands die.

Another common problem in visiting widows is the well-meaning intentions of people who make the empty offer, "If there is anything I can do, just call." The fact is that most widows will not call if they happen to remember in their state of grief who made the offer in the first place. Words without actions are meaningless to a widow. When she hears, "We would like to have you over sometime," and yet an invitation never occurs, the widow often becomes angry and disappointed with hollow promises.

Sometimes we miss the obvious in properly visiting widows. If a woman did not change the oil or tune the family automobile when her husband was alive, what makes us think that she is capable of performing car maintenance now? If her husband handled the family finances, wrote checks, paid the bills, and reconciled the bank statements, why should we assume she is competent to take care of these matters in her widowhood? If a widow could not afford to hire someone to mow her lawn or remove snow from her walks when her husband was alive, why would she necessarily be able to afford to do it now?

True spirituality is not measured by faithful attendance to meetings, academic knowledge of doctrine, or conforming to established human codes. James tells us that true reverence for God is demonstrated by visiting orphans and widows in practical ways.

Making It a Special Call

How can we effectively call on widows in their time of trouble? What can we do to maintain a regular visitation of widows long after the funerals are over? Is there any way in which we can equip people in the church to get involved in ministering to widows? A few suggestions may help to answer these questions.

The first step in effective visitation is to list the names of widows in your church and their addresses. I am always amazed at church leaders and laypersons who occasionally tell me they cannot think of a single widow in their churches. Once they ponder the matter, they begin to think of names of widows in their fellowships they have overlooked. The exercise of listing widows helps to identify exactly which widows in the church need to be contacted.

The next step in practical visitation is organization. An organized approach to visiting widows in a local church may be accomplished in a variety of ways. Deacons and their spouses may volunteer to be responsible for one or more widows in the church. These leaders may agree to visit their widows at least twice a year to determine needs and ways to address these needs.

Our church conducts a weekly visitation ministry in which widows are often included on the list and are visited by laypersons. It is important to train laypersons to tune in to the needs of these widows during such visits and to communicate any needs to those in the church who may be able to help. Appendix A is a sample widows visitation report which might serve as a tool in addressing the needs of widows in a local church.

The church's care givers need to include visitation to widows as part of their ministry. Many of these women look to the church in their time of need to help them through the bereavement period. It must not abandon them with the passing of time. Once they settle into their new role as widows, the need for counsel may actually increase.

I discovered that when leaders are concerned about widows, their concern pulsates throughout the entire church body. It is as if people begin to wake up after a long night's sleep to the needs of widows. In the early church (Acts 6:1–6), if leaders (the apostles) had not taken the initiative to care for widows, the neglect would have continued, just as it will in our churches today if leaders fail to respond to the problem of caring for widows.

One of the most valuable human resources to visit widows in meaningful ways is found in other widows. Phyllis Silverman, a pioneer in widow research, made a significant discovery concerning the recovery of the newly widowed. She concluded that the newly widowed woman would be more apt to open herself up to another widow than to a mental-health professional or any other care giver. She explains her conclusion in the following:

> Help from a peer has no stigma and does not have to be defined as help. It has the quality of neighborly interest which includes the opportunity to reciprocate. The helper in this context provides a role model, friendship, some guidance, and is a bridge person facilitating the new widow's reintegration into the broader community.[1]

Widows who have successfully managed their own grief provide some of the most effective care to other women who are entering this new world of widowhood. Churches need to equip veteran widows to constructively fulfill the role of ministering to those who share in their plight.

Networking widows to other persons who may be better able to meet their specific needs is yet another practical way to visit widows in their distress. Widows may need the legal assistance of a competent attorney. Church members can offer valuable help by connecting them with reputable attorneys in the community. Perhaps widows require other services from an accountant, physician, counselor, or banker. A "yellow pages" of services could be developed by a local church to network widows to trustworthy services and professionals.

Professionals such as attorneys, physicians, accountants, clergymen, bankers, and business people in the church can assist widows beyond their normal practices. Realizing the financial difficulties many widows face, professionals may give courtesy discounts to widows they serve. One man who owns a lubrication business in our city takes it upon himself to regularly service without charge the automobile of one of the widows of our church who lives in his apartment complex.

Lee knew that his friend Spike was dying. He learned that Spike's family car and a pickup truck were only registered in his name and not in joint tenancy of ownership with his wife Delores. If Spike died with the vehicles registered only in his name, it would be more difficult for his wife to secure the vehicles without extra legal costs to free them from the estate. Lee networked Spike to a notary public by bringing the notary to Spike's residence to change the titles of the vehicles to the status of joint tenancy of ownership. When Spike died, the vehicles automatically transferred to Delores's ownership.

One other example will illustrate how professionals can assist widows. Ed is an insurance agent. He insured a very close friend of his who ended his own life shortly after he had changed life insurance policies. Since the policy contained a "suicide clause," it appeared that the widow would receive no benefits from the policy.

Ed, a committed Christian businessman, believed the insurance company should listen to the extenuating circumstances of this case and award the widow the insurance money. Acting on her behalf and at his own expense, the agent flew to California to plead the case of this widow before an appeals board. The result of his efforts proved triumphant, as the board agreed with him and decided to issue the life insurance proceeds to the widow. In one sense the agent had a professional obligation to intervene for the widow in this situation, but he was motivated by a greater sense of obligation. He was driven by the biblical motive of visiting a widow in her trouble.

A systematic approach to visitation should be adopted by the local church to assure that no widow is neglected in that particular fellowship. To assure that a call is a special visit, it must address both the felt and actual needs of widows.

Summary

Most churches, regardless of size or location, have widows in their ranks. Unfortunately, many widows say they receive only temporary support from their church. They are often forgotten after the first year. In this affluent, independent society, congregations may be tempted to assign the care of widows to social agencies, government programs, and secular professionals.

From God's perspective, visiting widows includes more than a mere social call. It means that Christians will personally get involved in the lives of widows in practical ways to meet their needs. Judi Stewart, former director of the widow-to-widow ministry at Hinson Memorial Baptist Church in Portland, Oregon, brags about her adult Sunday school class. "My class was extremely supportive during my loss. Each year, one of the adult Sunday school classes designates a month when the members of the class volunteer to help widows with household chores that widows like myself can neither afford to have done nor do themselves. Some men from the class helped me move some heavy furniture from my attic."

Another way a church can care for its widows, Judi says, is to help them with their children. "Most widows appreciate the positive male role models that the men of the church can provide." Although no one can replace a deceased father, men can play a meaningful part in children's lives by taking them camping, accompanying them to athletic events, teaching mechanical skills, and building relationships through traditional father-child activities.

Once the church returns to a biblical priority of "visiting" widows in their distress, it will experience the rich blessing of God. Visiting widows is one of the practical ways we can please God.

One of the most meaningful activities widows in the church can perform is that of helping other widows through their grief and with their needs. No one really understands the heart and soul of a widow as does another widow.

Questions for Discussion

1. Why is caring for widows so important to God?

2. Why should the church be involved in the lives of widows in practical ways?

3. What are some of the ways your fellowship is presently visiting widows in the sense of James 1:27?

4. How could your church improve its ministry to widows?

5. How would you evaluate your personal involvement in visiting the widows of your church or community? How would you evaluate the involvement of your church leaders? How would you evaluate the involvement of widows in your church visiting other widows?

6. What kind of changes would occur in your church if the members began visiting widows in the biblical style of James 1:27?

Application

1. Resolve to visit at least one widow in your church who may not have family nearby. In your visit, attempt to discover some practical needs she can neither afford to have resolved nor is able to resolve herself.

2. Arrange to meet the need of the widow you visited by either tending to it yourself or networking the task with someone in the church who is capable of fulfilling the need.

3. Enlist and equip a group of widows in the church who may be able to call on recent widows.

4. Designate a month in the church calendar where church members volunteer to help widows with household chores that they can neither afford to have done nor do themselves.

5. Remember a widow in your congregation by a thoughtful act such as sending a valentine, birthday, or anniversary card, or an invitation to dinner.

4 Coping with Emotional Pain

੭৶

"NUMB IS TRULY the word. I felt as though I had been given a massive dose of emotional novocaine right after the doctor phoned to tell me that Sam had died."[1] These are the words of one widow who speaks for many widows in their assessment of the initial moments following the deaths of their husbands.

Why Does It Hurt So Much?

This first stage of emotional pain is called grief. Grief is a series of painful emotions and experiences into which a person enters and lives for a period of time that begins with significant changes, losses, and life transitions. The emotional reaction to a significant loss takes on many characteristics. Like physical pain, emotional pain is not visible. It is impossible for people to fully understand what another person is feeling during personal grief. This lack of understanding may lead to some erroneous conclusions about the nature of grief.

Myths about Grief

People hold strong opinions about how others should respond to irrevocable losses. Insensitive statements such as, "She should be over it by now," or, "It has already been one year since he died; she should be pulling herself together," or, "She is merely feeling sorry for herself" are often heard by grieving widows. The basis for these hurtful statements is founded in faulty assumptions—myths—which some people have about grief.

Myth 1: Grief Is Limited by Time

One common misconception about grief is that it is resolved within a definite time. Some see one year after the loss of a spouse as the normal period of time in which the widow should recover from her grief. Customs related to passages of mourning (funerals, burials, etc.) and cultural expectations often dictate the time frame in which this emotional pain is expected to cease. The widow's emotional pain is intensified by insensitive care givers who believe her time of grief is up.

Myth 2: Grief Has Systematic Stages

There are stages of grief: numbness, denial, anger, guilt. Some people think that a widow will automatically experience these phases in a chronological order. Lynn Caine writes from both her own experience as a widow and that of hundreds of other women by warning against locking women into a set pattern and timetable for grief:

> Each woman responds to the death of her husband in her own way. The stages of grief can overlap or be jumbled

together, or they can show up in an order different from the way they are presented here. There is no such thing as normal grief and no set timetable for passing through each of its phases.[2]

Myth 3: Grief Is Abnormal

Most people accept a widow's grief as being normal for a brief duration. Soon after the funeral of the deceased, many friends and relatives of the widow begin to feel uncomfortable around her. They do not understand why she desires to talk about her late partner or why she begins to cry in the middle of a church service. These and other similar actions from the widow are interpreted as abnormal behavior.

This perception of abnormality may cause friends and family members to intervene in a widow's grief because they do not want to see her hurt. But grief becomes abnormal only when it is repressed and denied. Delayed grief in the life of a widow will have damaging emotional consequences. "Do not tamper with a widow's grief" is the best recommendation to these well-meaning people who want to help her.

Myth 4: Grief Should Be Sedated

"I have a friend who can give you some prescription drugs to calm you." A woman spoke to a widow who had just received news of the accidental death of her husband. The use of tranquilizers, antidepressants, and sedatives are commonly believed to help a woman in her grief, especially during the initial stage of her bereavement.

Drugs become a straitjacket around the emotions of

women who are sedated during sorrow. Widows are unable to grieve as they desire if they are hindered by sedatives. The blockage of emotional pain by drugs can actually contribute to a slower recovery. Studies suggest that such drugs do little to improve coping with bereavement.[3]

Myth 5: Grief Is More Severe with Sudden Deaths

Widows whose husbands die without warning argue that their grief is worse because they did not have a chance to prepare for grief. On the other hand, widows who watched their husbands suffer terminal diseases contend that their grief is more intense because they had to endure the emotional pain of watching their loved ones suffer.

Caine emphasizes the value of understanding what each widow experiences in either the sudden death of her spouse or the long-expected death. She also cautions against promoting competition among widows as to which type of death is worse for grief:

> There is value, I think, in recognizing what a woman faces when she must watch her husband die slowly over many months, as I did, and in understanding the intensified shock that comes from sudden death, when a woman's husband leaves for work in the morning and never arrives there. What rule of measurement can judge which of these is worse? None.[4]

Myth 6: Grief Is Easier for Younger Widows

Some conclude that because a younger widow has not been married as long as her older counterpart, her grief may not be as painful. It must be underscored that grief is essentially the same for widows regardless of their age. Younger widows may grieve over different issues from those of older widows, but their pain is not less.

There are two reasons why it hurts so much to grieve. First, the necessary pain of grief purges sorrow from a person. Unlike a true illness, grief actually has healing powers. A widow needs to cry in her expression of grief. She needs to take the painful steps of planning her husband's funeral and thereby take an active role in the grieving process. The widow cannot heal emotionally from her loss until she experiences the painful process of grief. In short, grief hurts because it heals.

Second, grief hurts because of the uninformed attitudes and insensitive actions of those who attempt to assist the grieving. This adds the burdens of self-doubt and guilt. The very nature of grief hurts enough without heaping on it incorrect expectations from care givers.

Those who minister to widows must exercise great care to avoid wrong ideas about grief. It is, therefore, important to understand some basic concepts of grief and how long a widow may experience such hurt.

How Long Does It Last?

There is a sense in which a widow may never get over the pain of her separation, but the pain does diminish. We must always remember that grief does not have set time limits.

The initial stage of grief is a period of shock. The Lord has designed our bodies with a built-in protective device that takes over in tragedy. Everything goes into a state of unreality at this point in grief. The widow almost unconsciously contacts relatives and friends about her husband's death. She goes through the days before, during, and after the funeral in a daze.

"A widow during her initial grief often is not capable of making some of the most simple decisions in her day-to-day functioning," Judi Stewart explained to me in personal conversation. "I could not make any decisions regarding shopping, paying bills, or going places for the first six months of my widowhood."

It is at this level of grief that a widow needs care givers who can objectively coach her to make sound decisions, or in some cases to postpone decisions until she is in a better frame of mind. How long does this initial stage last? Stewart testifies that she experienced this phase for six months. Other widows may go an entire year through this impact stage of grief.

Eventually, widows move into another stage of grief referred to as the recoil stage. This is a time when the widow begins to experience a gyration of the emotions of anger, denial, guilt, idealization, and depression. After two years of widowhood, Delores said to me, "Pastor, I still have times when I feel like I am losing my mind."

How long does the recoil stage last? Again, no timetable can be established. Some widows have reported remaining at this level in their grief for five years. The important thing to remember is that whatever time this stage takes, it is necessary and normal to experience the various emotional seasons of grief. A widow should not panic if she has relapses of feelings she thought she had put behind her. Care givers should not be concerned if a widow is not recovering from grief as quickly as they think she should.

The last stage of grief is sometimes called the accommodation stage. In it the widow makes a successful reentry into society in her new role as a widow. It is in this period that a widow usually remains indefinitely. This final stage of grief is marked by recurrence of those emotions experienced in the recoil stage but to a lesser degree. One of the most lingering feelings experienced by widows at this stage of grief is loneliness.

Alone Again

The very reason God brought man and woman together into marriage was for companionship (Gen. 2:18). When death breaks this union, an inevitable void forms. The widow knows that part of her life is gone.

Loneliness is one of the extended by-products of grief for a widow. Like a low-grade headache, loneliness continues to afflict widows long after the other emotional components of grief are discontinued.

"We have discovered that Sunday afternoons are one of the loneliest times of the week for many widows," Judi Stewart explains. "For this reason we schedule our widow-to-widow meeting times at Hinson from 4:00 to 5:45 P.M. on Sundays."

On the average, a woman remains in the state of widowhood for eighteen years of her life.[5] The wilderness experience of loneliness often spans the entire time. It is a primary problem of widowhood which requires careful attention by both widows themselves and care givers.

Pitfalls of Loneliness

A lonely widow can often be an angry widow. This anger is different from the kind she experiences during the grieving process (e.g., becoming angry at her husband because he did not take care of his health, which resulted in his death). Lonely anger is characterized by endless dissatisfaction and antagonism. A widow who has fallen into this trap alienates herself from those friends and relatives who could be a comfort to her. She is caught between desiring more friends to pacify her loneliness and driving these same friends away by her angry attitudes and actions.

Loneliness can also lead to isolation. Widows may fall into the rut of withdrawing from church gatherings, social events, and intimate friendships because personal loneliness cannot be expressed and must be carried alone. There is one worse thing than being alone and lonely: being surrounded by a crowd of people and still feeling lonely.

Insecurity can be another danger in loneliness. Loneliness is created by the loss of a companion, lover, and provider. It is magnified when widows drive close friends and relatives away because of anger. When these security supports have been removed, the widow experiences more insecurity.

Fighting Loneliness

Most widows agree that one of the first steps in recovering from loneliness is to face this emotion directly. Widows need to feel the pain of loneliness, which will drive them to seek the cure. The cure consists of a few techniques that will require time to work.

Useful activities will benefit the widow in fighting loneliness. Volunteer work, continued education, or employment are a few activities that can increase a widow's own self-worth as well as contribute to society by her participation.

Developing new roles and relationships is another solution to the problem of loneliness. A widow may be able to develop her grandmother role to occupy her time. She may join civic groups or other organizations, which introduces her to a new class of friends and takes the bite out of loneliness.

Some widows give themselves to a cause that is not only rewarding but also eases their loneliness. Political issues, educational matters, economic concerns, and spiritual interests are a few of the many causes widows may focus on to broaden their social roles.

Our church hosted a panel discussion on volunteerism for the widows in our community. The directors of volunteer services from the two hospitals in our city explained to the women what services were available, how to apply for a volunteer position, and the rewards of volunteering. Most cities have abundant opportunities for volunteer work through which widows can combat loneliness.

How to Help Ease the Pain

Most grief management will occur from the pastoral care ministry of a local church. Howard Clinebell states, "Ministers are the only professional persons with training in counseling who have automatic entree to the world of sorrowing people." He adds, "Obviously, it behooves pastors to develop a high degree of competence in bereavement care and counseling."[6]

Laypersons can be trained to support widows through their passages of grief and thereby relieve the pastor from bearing the entire weight of this support. Churches throughout the world host seminars and encourage their people to attend international conferences sponsored by the International Lay Pastoral Care Ministry. This ministry for laypersons is based in the Hope Presbyterian Church, Richfield, Minnesota.[7]

Doris Sanford, cofounder of the widow-to-widow ministry at Hinson Baptist Church, planned a creative seminar to educate the congregation about grief and widowhood. "I arranged to have a casket placed at the front of the sanctuary," she says. "Then I turned the lights out, with only a spotlight shining upon the casket." Next, Sanford called approximately 85 percent of the men from the audience to gather around the casket, explaining that 85 percent of married women will be widowed.

Care givers can learn some valuable lessons from Job's friends, who immediately responded to his grief by entering into grief with him (Job 2:11–13). The Bible says that these friends sat with Job for seven days and nights not uttering a word. They knew that Job's emotional pain was so acute that nervous chattering, the giving of pat answers, or the offering of trite clichés would not help him during his initial stage of grief. They merely sat and listened if Job wished to talk. "Blessed is that congregation that has a pastor who knows how to keep his mouth shut and his ears open to the *feelings* expressed by the words spoken," say Warren and David Wiersbe.[8]

As Job's friends were with him, it is also important for those who care to be with the grieving widow in her time of need. Initially, people are usually good about sitting with a widow, at least until the funeral is over. A few close friends may continue to be with the widow a few months after the funeral, but later the widow often finds herself facing grief alone.

One of our widows testified to several other widows that she had gone over to another widow's home to spend the night with her because she was afraid of being alone. "I would actually sleep with her like I would with a frightened child," Loreen explained. "As long as she could reach over and feel my hand, the widow would go back to sleep." Loreen stated that she had to sleep this way for two weeks until the new widow overcame the fear of being alone at night.

There are three difficult times in the seasons of a widow's life that care givers must especially understand. The first anniversary of the death is particularly hard, since all of the memories of the death and the loss will most likely be recalled by the widow. Holidays are also difficult times for widows. Christmas, Easter, Father's Day, and other special times that were shared by the husband and wife will now become hollow for many widows. The final difficult time in widowhood is the wedding anniversary. The celebration of wedding anniversaries of close friends also will painfully remind widows of their losses.

Widows feel care at a very personal level when they receive a birthday card, valentine, or a token gift for their wedding anniversary. Those yearly milestones are especially difficult after a husband's death.

Many specific ideas of how to assist widows in their recovery from grief can be developed creatively. Again, understanding, gentleness, and practical action are the ingredients which go into the prescription for helping ease the emotional pain widows experience.

Summary

The emotional pain of grief hurts intensely when a major part of a woman's life, her husband, has been removed from her life. No other life event has a more negative impact on a woman than the loss of her husband through death.

Long after the other phases of grief have passed, the widow continues to experience loneliness. Loneliness can actually be positive when a widow is driven to seek companionship with the Lord. The spiritual values resulting from loneliness make the pain bearable. After they have been alone for some time, widows often testify that they pray more, read the Bible more, trust more, and enjoy the fellowship of other believers more.

To properly care for those experiencing grief, a clear working knowledge of the nature of grief, of how to manage grief, and a sensitivity toward widows experiencing grief are vital. The myths of grief must be dispelled if a widow's emotional pain is expected to decline. When both care givers and widows work in concert to address the pain of grief, healing will result.

Questions for Discussion

1. What lessons can we learn from Job's friends for helping someone during personal grief (see Job 2)?

2. Why do a number of professional care givers (clergymen, funeral directors, counselors, etc.), feel ill-equipped to help people through grief? How can both professionals and laypersons become better equipped to assist in grief management?

3. Why does the emotional pain of losing a spouse hurt so much compared with other negative life events? How does Genesis 2:18 help to explain the pain of grief in a widow?

4. What are some of the factors that cause loneliness in the life of a widow? How can she combat loneliness? How can her family or church assist her through loneliness?

5. How can a widow successfully recover from her grief?

Application

1. Read *Don't Take My Grief Away* by Doug Manning. After reading the book, outline the stages of grief and a brief description of each stage.

2. Accompany your pastor or another care giver on a visit to a grieving widow. Observe those actions and words which were either a help or a hindrance in assisting the woman in grief. After the visit, record your observations.

3. Attend a seminar in your area sponsored by a local hospital, funeral home, or church on how to help people through grief.

4. Send a card, a token gift, or flowers to a widow in remembrance of a special day in her life.

5. Plan a creative seminar in your church to educate the congregation about grief and widowhood.

5   Caring for the Widow's Health

è∎

THERAPISTS AGREE in ranking the onset of widow-hood as one of the most stressful life events women experience. A widow's health is at a higher risk of declining during the first few years of widowhood than at any other time in her life. The emotional trauma of widowhood triggers negative physical effects for widows. If widows are going to be successful in their fight against poor health, both widows and care givers will need to discover the symptoms of and remedies for ill health.

Symptoms

Increased illness among widows after their losses is measured in several ways. One way is to note the increased visits to doctors by widows. Another way is to observe their physical appearance. Weight and hair loss, skin irritations, and nervousness are a few of the physical signs of deteriorating health. Yet another way is to listen to the increased complaints of widows themselves. Complaints of fatigue, insomnia, and loss of appetite represent some of the physical problems mentioned by widows.

Heart disease is the most common symptom to plague a woman after she loses her husband.[1] "Three months after my husband died, my heart blew up," Betty told me. "Five months later, I required open heart surgery." Prior to her husband's death, she had never experienced heart trouble. Betty's doctors recognized stress as the contributing cause to her heart problems. The emotional stress of losing her husband had provoked serious health difficulties.

Widows are more prone to cancer, infectious diseases, accidents, suicides, cirrhosis, and alcoholism.[2] These health problems escalate when they become the source of more worry to add to worries the widows already have.

The physical well-being of a widow affects her psychological or mental health. Symptoms such as depression, paranoia, fear, poor self-esteem, and suicidal thoughts reflect declining mental wellness. Psychologists recognize a higher incident rate of psychological problems among widows compared with other segments of society.

One in three widows increases her consumption of drugs such as sedatives and tranquilizers after the loss of her husband.[3] In some situations there is a seven-fold increase in the prescription of sedatives in the first six months following bereavement for patients under age sixty-five. Increased smoking among one in nine widows is found in one study.[4]

The Prescription

One of the first actions a widow should be encouraged to take is to schedule a complete physical examination with a reputable physician. This examination should be completed within the initial year of bereavement to detect any early symptoms which can be treated immediately.

Information about pulse rate, blood pressure, heart action, condition of eyes and ears, and other parts of a woman's body may be valuable in preventing some serious health problems in the future. Since most widows are in such a state of grief that they probably will not consider scheduling a physical exam, it would be helpful if relatives or friends would encourage these needy women in this matter.

Another action a widow can take to help in her fight against poor health is to get adequate rest. Authors Donald and Rita Cushenbery say that "the most common complaint of grieving spouses is difficulty in establishing a regular pattern of restful sleep."[5] Practical matters of where one sleeps, the quality of pillows, the atmosphere of the room, and preliminary preparations for a good night's sleep (such as taking a warm bath or shower before bed, mild exercise before bedtime, or simply slowing down activities at least an hour before sleep), should be considered by widows who need to deal with insomnia.

A proper diet is also critical to both the physical and mental health of a widow. Cooking for one will tempt a widow to skip meals or to snack during irregular hours. Two extreme tendencies are to either overeat or undereat.

Recently, my wife and I were invited to the home of a widow for Sunday dinner. She prepared a feast. I justified my gluttony that day by thinking I gave her a good reason to eat a balanced meal for a change. But seriously, if widows regularly invite people over for a meal, they will satisfy both their nutritional and social needs.

Many widows dread the dinner hour because they feel they no longer have a reason to cook. Philomene Gates recommends, "Set aside a time with 'real' food that you've cooked yourself; eat at the kitchen or dining table set with nice dishes and a flower or candle. This is a psychological and nutritional necessity."[6]

A contributing factor to a healthy body is proper exercise. Exercise is an excellent antidote to relieving stress. Walking, swimming, bicycling, and aerobics are a few exercises which can benefit a widow's health. Widows need to get friends to accompany them in a chosen exercise if they do not like to work out alone.

There are also prescriptions to maintain good mental health. A personal faith in Jesus Christ is the only enduring resource for maintaining a healthy mental condition. Psalm 146:9 says that God "sustains the fatherless and widow." To sustain a widow means that God will nourish or support her in every need. This truth applies to the psychological needs of a widow as well.

The Christian widow has the distinct advantage of memorizing appropriate scriptural promises, praying during the dark times of her grief, and surrounding herself with the love of the Lord's people to safeguard her physical and mental health.

The End of a Love Life

The subject of sex in widowhood is usually avoided in Christian literature, and it often is treated in a very unbiblical and immoral way in secular literature. However, just because death terminates the physical relationship between a husband and wife does not mean that the sexual and affectional desires of the widow cease.

The apostle Paul speaks to this practical, physical problem of widowhood: "Now to the unmarried and widows

I say: It is good for them to stay unmarried as I am. But if they cannot control themselves, they should marry, for it is better to marry than to burn with passion" (1 Cor. 7:8–9).

God's plan for sex is limited to marriage. Illicit sex violates God's plan and will cause conflict in the spiritual life of a widow. A widow's sexual drive must be governed by divine directives, personal discipline, and a willingness to "learn to control [her] own body in a way that is holy and honorable, not in passionate lust like the heathen, who do not know God" (1 Thess. 4:4–5).

Widows have affectional needs besides sex. "I miss a male giving me a hug," Eleanor says. "When some of the men of my church greet me at church with a hug, a tremendous need is being met in my life." These affectional needs should not be interpreted as sinful.

Those of us who are associated with widows need to show tangible and tasteful expressions of affection toward them. The early New Testament believers demonstrated physical expressions of feeling in their relationships with one another with the "holy kiss" and embraces. The Lord created us as people who require affection. When widows lose their primary source of human affection in the persons of their husbands, it becomes necessary for other care givers to step in and show as much Christian love as possible.

Some cautions in expressing tasteful affection toward widows from men should be mentioned, lest there are misunderstandings. These physical expressions should be clearly perceived as brotherly love. Professional care givers need to exercise the same caution they would ordinarily follow with any other woman they might assist. They must take care that they "do not allow what you consider good to be spoken of as evil" (Rom. 14:16).

Widows need to know what God's Word says about their sexuality now that their spouses are gone. There will be incredible sexual pressure upon women, especially in our present promiscuous and relativistic society. Biblical counsel will be required in some cases to help widows to understand how to cope with their individual sexuality.

Summary

The widow's fight in health care is one of survival and maintenance. Her friends will need to encourage her, especially during the first year, to take care of herself. Physicians should request any of their recently widowed patients to come in for a thorough checkup. During the first year of bereavement it is critical to monitor a widow's health.

A regular, well-balanced diet will be a contributing factor to a widow's physical health. Restful sleep, adequate exercise, and a positive mental attitude are also essential building blocks in the health of a widow.

Who cares about the health of the widow? The widow herself should care. Next, those who are concerned about her as a person should care and make sure she remains healthy.

Family, friends, and professional care givers need to be sensitive to the sexual and affectional cravings of widows. They must not avoid acknowledging the real physical desires a widow has. These desires must be addressed from a biblical perspective, with warnings to widows of the dangers in illicitly satisfying their sexual appetites.

Questions for Discussion

1. Why are widows at a higher risk of losing their health than they were prior to their husbands' deaths?

2. What are the biblical reasons against recreational sex or sex outside of marriage?

3. What guidelines should we follow in showing physical affection while avoiding sexual indiscretions?

4. As a leader in a local church, how would you approach a situation where you discovered one of the widows in your church was living in immorality?

5. What are some ways we can assist widows in strengthening their mental well-being?

Application

1. List some of the reliable doctors in your community who may be called on by widows for health care.

2. Schedule special speakers from the health care community to address different health issues with the widows of your church.

3. Prepare and teach a Bible lesson on the subject of sexual purity for singles.

4. Record some appropriate expressions of affection that might be communicated to the widows in your church. Identify the widows in your church who might appreciate a hug or a special touch and give one.

5. Organize special activities which will provide moderate physical exercise for the widows of your community.

6 Managing the Widow's Mites

ཟ

A WOMAN'S INCOME level automatically drops by 40 percent when she loses the financial support of her late husband.[1] I conducted a survey among the widows of our community by asking them to list the five greatest fears they have in widowhood. An overwhelming majority of the respondents listed financial fears as one of their chief concerns. Some responses were "I fear not having enough to make ends meet," "I worry about losing my house because of upkeep costs," or "My concern is not having enough money when my health deteriorates."

Widows face two basic financial concerns when they lose their primary source of support. (1) If a widow does not have enough money to survive, then her concern will be to get sufficient income to subsist; and (2) if the widow does have plenty of money, then the concerns are for protecting and managing her assets so the supply will last until her death.

Providing for Financial Needs

Thankfully, few widows have financial needs as dramatic as did Martha, the Vietnamese widow who depended on roadkill for food. Yet many of the homeless in our land include widows who eat scraps out of dumpsters from fast-food restaurants or appear at rescue missions to eat at least one balanced meal during the day.

One study showed that within a year after their husbands died, 37 percent of surviving widows who previously had not been poor had fallen below the poverty line.[2] Poverty in widowhood is a major problem which churches need to recognize.

Preparation

The proverbial saying "An ounce of prevention is worth a pound of cure" certainly applies to the financial provision for widows. Pastors and church leaders make a major contribution toward easing the financial burdens of prospective widows when they influence husbands to plan early and properly for their eventual deaths.

Lynn Caine suggests a "contingency day" for couples, when they prepare for the husband's death to avoid potential financial struggles in the future. A contingency day would be the couple's annual review of their financial status. On this particular day the couple would discuss steps to be taken if either husband or wife should die. If the wife were to be widowed that year, she would have the security of knowing what debts were outstanding, what her assets were (including stocks, bonds, certificates of deposit, real estate, and bank accounts), what her life insurance policy meant in dollars and cents, and what would be her government benefits.[3]

It is especially important for women whose husbands own their own businesses to acquaint themselves with these enterprises before they are widowed. More than one widow in this situation has said that if she had it to do all over again, she would become more involved in her husband's business earlier and would ask more questions.

Appendix B introduces one of the most recent resources available for families to use in preparing for sudden illness, death, or other catastrophe which might threaten the future of a family-owned business. *Preparing . . . Just in Case* is a detailed workbook which may be obtained through the Family Business Program at Oregon State University. The husband fills out the information, and then both the husband and wife go over it together to make sure the wife understands every detail. If her husband is a business owner and dies, the survival of the business may depend on her having this vital information.

Most family-business owners are men, and women tend to outlive men by about five years.[4] It only makes sense for a woman to consider ahead of time what will happen to the business after her husband dies. The preservation and continuation of a business may be critical for the future financial security of a widow. Women would have a great advantage in their widowhood if before their husbands die they would become actively involved in the companies and remain fully informed about the businesses.

Most women will not require detailed business information when they are widowed, but a contingency day is still recommended for couples at any income level. Simple financial matters such as writing checks, paying outstanding bills, balancing the family checkbook, and a number of other personal financial duties should be learned by women before they are widowed.

Immediate Help

Even when the proceeds from life insurance, Social Security, or investment income will adequately provide for them, the process of collecting those resources takes time. Some women may not have enough money to buy a loaf of bread during the first weeks of their widowhood.

"When my husband passed away, I did not have one cent to purchase groceries for the week," Tillie confided. "If it were not for a close friend who offered me a $500 loan right after my husband died, I do not know what I would have done."

A local church should be sensitive to this type of situation by offering an immediate, interest-free loan for the cash needed to assist a widow through the interim between her loss and the time she begins receiving her benefits. My church established a widows' fund, which is designed to offer such a loan or gift to widows who might experience a cash flow problem in the days following their husbands' deaths. Typically, most women are too ashamed or proud to admit their financial need, especially if they will have financial resources available in the future.

Financial counselor Larry Burkett encourages widows who experience immediate needs to "let the other Christians around you know that you have needs—and be specific."[5] Most Christians will respond and help widows who have need. I tell the widows at Emmanuel that none of us is the fourth member of the Trinity—all-knowing. If they have needs, they must be willing to come forward with that information.

Delores discovered she needed to put in a new septic system on her property. The cost of this necessity was over $2,000. She did not have the money but was forced to have the work done. She called me at the church and informed me that she was going to go to the credit union and secure a loan for the system. I asked her to delay her appointment to the credit union until she at least made the financial need known to the members of Emmanuel and gave them the opportunity to pray with her about the situation. The result was that a significant portion of the total cost of the project was contributed by the members, the Lord provided some other unexpected funds for Delores, and the contractor was willing to work with her on the remaining balance.

The immediate needs of widows may not always translate into actual cash. Service needs such as mechanical work on automobiles, tax preparation, carpentry work, and other similar labor can result in financial demands on widows. Rather than merely give money, Christians may assist by offering their skills and services to widows who would otherwise have to hire someone they may not be able to afford.

Protecting Financial Assets

Some women may actually become prosperous when they lose their husbands through death. Occasionally, some wives remind their husbands that as widows, they would be better off financially.

Prosperity may result from large insurance proceeds, family businesses having all debts relieved because of insurance, or a home that is automatically paid in full when death occurs. Admittedly, widows who are left with substantial income do not struggle economically like those who are left with very little. The affluent widow will, however, have some concerns related to her wealth.

The Life Insurance and Marketing Association points

out that one of every four widows exhausts her husband's life insurance within two years of his death.[6] "If a new widow does not complete even a basic financial plan within six weeks of her husband's death, she is in grave danger of spending her entire inheritance," warns Charlotte Kirsch, author of *A Survival Manual.*[7]

Protecting a widow's assets from eroding through poor investments, scams, and other financial pitfalls becomes the major objective in assisting her. Horror stories abound about widows who have lost everything they owned through poor planning or no planning.

Larry Burkett tells widows that the "single most important decision that any recent widow can make is to make no decision—whether about investments, loans, new cars, or anything else that might jeopardize her assets—for at least one year."[8] A widow should concentrate on coping with her grief, adjusting to a new life, and becoming educated on the ins and outs of money management during her first year.

Care givers can provide considerable service to a widow who needs to protect her assets for her future livelihood. This service may begin by networking her to a team of professionals who will offer sound financial counsel.

Developing a Team

Proverbs 11:14 states: "For lack of guidance a nation falls, but many advisers make victory sure." Developing a team of trustworthy professionals to assist widows in protecting their assets may provide such financial safety.

Four essential personnel can be employed to assist widows in protecting their holdings. All four may not be necessary for widows who have little inheritance, but one of these professionals may be necessary from time to time for simple matters.

Insurance Agent

The first to be considered is a reputable life insurance agent. The life insurance agent is one of the few professionals involved in the life of a widow who is actually able to bring good news: that there are adequate benefits from a life insurance policy. An agent who is genuinely interested in the financial welfare of the new widow can assist her in placing the lump sum benefits for one year into a savings account or money fund.

A reputable insurance agent is also competent in recommending the kind of insurance coverage that the widow herself should consider, since her life has changed to a single status. It is suggested that a wife become acquainted with the family insurance agent before she is widowed to establish a confident relationship for the future.

Several factors should be considered when selecting a life insurance counselor to protect a widow's assets. The agent should have an established track record with clients who can attest to qualified performance. The integrity of the agent should also be considered. Questions like, "Is the agent concerned about the welfare of the widow, or merely for his own profit?" need to be asked. A final factor might include the level of comfort a widow feels when dealing with her agent. Her husband may have had a close working relationship with a particular agent, but the widow does not share that same bond. A widow should not feel guilty hiring another agent if she does not feel comfortable with the one her late husband had employed.

Attorney

The second key member to join a widow's team should be a reliable attorney. Since attorneys, like doctors, specialize in different areas, it is important to secure a lawyer who is trained in estate and tax matters. A widow might ask her friends (especially those who are widowed) about certain attorneys. She may also consult a legal referral service or go to her local library and check with the *Martindale-Hubbel Law Directory,* which lists attorneys by city, state, and educational background. It is not out of order for a widow to interview more than one attorney before making her choice. This interview should disclose the fees, billing procedures, and who will be doing the bulk of the required legal work—the lawyer, an associate, or a paralegal.[9]

Accountant

The third member who should be included on the widow's professional team is a certified public accountant. A good accountant can assist by filing timely tax information for the widow to avoid penalties, taking advantage of tax breaks available to the widow, and advising her in future tax-related matters.

Financial Planner

The final member to be considered for this team is a financial planner. It must be underscored that this team member, like all the others previously mentioned, must have a reputable character. A financial planner may provide valuable assistance in developing a budget for the widow, coaching her on where to safely invest her money, and helping her with other financial questions.

The reason for this financial team concept is that all four professionals provide a check and balance on each other. Ultimately, the widow must make her own financial decisions, but she will cut her economic risks by surrounding herself with the counsel of capable professionals represented in these four financial areas.

Summary

Finances may be one of the most fundamental needs found in widowhood. Widows may need provision if they are left in financial distress because of insufficient income; or they may need protection of their assets from erosion because of a lack of planning or poor recommendations.

Husbands can make it easier on their wives by preparing them financially before they are widowed. This can be done by including wives in the financial and business areas that will eventually be assumed by them. Both family and church members can assist a widow by encouraging her to postpone any major financial decisions for at least one year. This will provide time for her to grieve without financial distractions.

The financial concerns of widowhood can be effectively addressed by those professionals who are trained to assist widows with their fiscal struggles.

Questions for Discussion

1. Is it safe to assume that the average woman in America does not have adequate income after her husband dies? What might be some observable signs of such financial needs in a widow's life?

2. What could your church do to assist a widow in meeting her immediate financial challenges? Her long-term challenges?

3. Why is it equally important to be concerned for a wealthy widow as it is for a poor widow? How might their financial needs be similar? How might they be different?

4. What are the values of developing a team of professionals to counsel a widow in her financial matters? How would you answer the objection "It is too expensive to employ such a team"?

5. Why are finances a fundamental need of widowhood?

Application

1. Conduct a financial seminar with an emphasis on singles. Include the basics of check writing, balancing statements, budgeting, etc., in the curriculum.

2. As a couple, schedule a contingency day to discuss steps to be taken if either spouse should die.

3. If you own your own business, order *Preparing . . . Just in Case* (information in appendix B) and complete it with your spouse.

4. At your next church board meeting, discuss the possibility of establishing a special widows' fund to be used for the express purpose of assisting widows in their financial plight.

5. Develop a list of reputable attorneys, insurance agents, accountants, and financial consultants in your community who might be called on by widows for counsel.

7   *Marrying Again*

è♦

THE NATIONAL Council of Compensation Insurance recently published figures which indicate the following:

One out of two widows between ages 26 and 30 do not remarry.
Two out of three widows between ages 31 and 35 do not remarry.
Four out of five widows between ages 36 and 40 do not remarry.[1]

These statistics are higher for widows with children.

"Statistically, I have more of a chance of being bombed by a terrorist than I do of remarrying," one widow told me in an interview. However, all of these statistics disagree with those of Larry Burkett, who states that "nearly 90 percent of all widows will get remarried."[2]

Regardless of the mathematical probabilities of remarriage for widows, it is a critical issue within the broad subject of widowhood. Remarriage for widows is specifically addressed in the New Testament on two different occasions.

In his first letter to the Corinthian church, the apostle Paul writes: "A woman is bound to her husband as long as he lives. But if her husband dies, she is free to marry anyone she wishes, but he must belong to the Lord" (1 Cor.

7:39). Paul makes it clear that remarriage for a Christian widow is permissible. It is interesting to note that only widows are addressed throughout the Bible and not widowers. One person suggests that the reason the Bible does not speak about widowers is because widowers remarry and widows grieve. Perhaps a better explanation is that the woman traditionally outlived the man and was economically dependent on him.

The apostle continues his instructions regarding the remarriage of widows in 1 Timothy 5:14: "So I counsel younger widows to marry, to have children, to manage their homes and to give no opportunity for slander." Remarriage for a widow is certainly encouraged in the Bible, but certain qualifications must be considered by both the widow and those who counsel her in the matter: pastors, counselors, and family members.

"Re-Marital" Counsel

I shall never forget a pastoral theology class during my seminary days when a pastor who served as professor for the class was dealing with the issue of premarital counseling. The pastor told us that he had required a prominent theologian from the seminary to go through the same extensive premarital classes as a young couple who had never been married. The theologian had been widowed after several years of marriage, and he was going to marry a widow who also had been previously married for many years.

"The false assumption is that the experienced couple does not require the same intense premarital counseling as the first-time couple," the pastor lectured. "The fact of the matter is that the veteran couple probably needs the counsel more, because they will bring excess baggage from their previous marriages into the second marriage, which will require special counsel."

Any widow who is considering remarriage should insist on premarital counseling. Before a pastor ties the knot again for a widow, she and her future husband should receive wise counsel on the unique challenges of a second marriage and blended families.

Is He the Right One?

"How do I know for sure if this man is the right one for me to marry?" is a leading question for any widow considering remarriage to ask of herself. Paul mentions in two different verses of 1 Corinthians 7 that it would be more beneficial for a widow not to remarry: "Now to the unmarried and the widows I say: It is good for them to stay unmarried, as I am. But if they cannot control themselves, they should marry, for it is better to marry than to burn with passion" (1 Cor. 7:8–9). After telling a woman that she is free to remarry anyone she wishes (1 Cor. 7:39), Paul states, "In my judgment, she is happier if she stays as she is" (1 Cor. 7:40).

The apostle does not contradict himself but says that the ideal state for a widow is the single state if she is able to cope. If the circumstances and the personality of a widow motivate her to remarry, then she should get married. Miriam Nye asks, "Do you believe that continuing single is better than risking a disappointing marriage? Have you shown that you can appreciate and make the most of life, whether married or not?"[3]

The point a widow needs to understand in her consideration to remarry is that if she is not happy with herself in her single state, she may only complicate her problem by thinking that remarriage will make her happy. The bottom line is to determine the real reason for wanting to remarry.

The driving force for a decision to remarry must be spiritual. First Timothy 5:11 characterizes younger widows who go astray spiritually by stating "they want to marry." Again, Paul does not contradict what he already said in encouraging widows to remarry. He simply shows a contrast between a Christ-centered widow who can marry "anyone she wishes, but he must belong to the Lord" (1 Cor. 7:39), and the carnal-centered widow who disregards any spiritual considerations in her remarriage.

Once the widow has determined the will of God in her decision to remarry, she should begin to pray for the "right one" to come into her life. She also needs to communicate her availability in tasteful ways. The most common complaint heard from widows who admit their interest in a second marriage is that it is difficult to meet eligible men and to communicate that they as widows are available.

A widow might consider removing her wedding ring for a starter. Many widows continue to wear their rings during the grieving process, but a time arrives when they are willing to remove these symbols of their previous unions and acknowledge a need to begin new lives.

Widows who are in search of husbands should adopt the attitude Abraham's servant had when he found a wife for Isaac: "and I bowed down and worshiped the LORD. I praised the LORD, the God of my master Abraham, who had led me on the right road to get the granddaughter of my master's brother for his son" (Gen. 24:48). Miriam Nye warns against using commercial methods in the search for a new husband by saying that "trying to 'make it happen' through aggressiveness, lonely hearts clubs, computer dating, and the like has proved disappointing for many."[4]

A wise principle to follow when looking for a new partner is to "look, but don't look like you're looking." What should you as a widow be looking for in the screening process for a new mate? Remember, Paul says, "he must belong to the Lord" (1 Cor. 7:39).

For a man to belong to the Lord means more than to be a professing Christian (which is important). The widow is to take into account the spiritual maturity of the prospective husband. Does he understand what it means to be a Christian leader in the home? Does he have a consistent walk with the Lord? What is his testimony to his own family members, his friends, his colleagues? If the widow has children, will he accept and love them as well as their mother?

Once these spiritual observations are made, the widow should make other important evaluations. The following list is not exhaustive but will provide some essential items to consider:

1. Do not compare with the first spouse.
2. Do not expect perfection.
3. Look for mutual interests.
4. Are religious and cultural backgrounds compatible?
5. Is there an openness and desire to grow together as husband and wife?
6. Is there an ability to communicate and to share decisions?
7. Note if the prospective husband is attracted to you as an individual rather than merely for your assets or physical beauty.
8. Look for financial stability in contrast to irresponsible fiscal attitudes.

A very important consideration in both deciding on re-marriage and exactly who the new husband might be is the children. If children are involved, a widow must consider their needs before she forces a new man into their lives. The children of widows may become formidable rivals to prospective partners. They may have an almost fierce loyalty to their deceased father and feel that they cannot betray him by accepting another "father." The mother should allow adequate time for children to develop a healthy friendship with the new man who may become part of their family.

The challenge of introducing a new father to children is great enough, but when the father is blending children of his own into the new relationship, the challenge becomes even greater. A widow must consider the long-term effects on her children if she allows the blend of rival siblings.

The will of the Lord is normally to provide a new spouse for the widow, but she must wait upon his guidance and follow the principles set forth in his Word to conform with his will. God will not lead a widow into a relationship that contradicts the teachings of his Word. The widow who desires to please the Lord in her decision to remarry will make a careful study of marriage in the Bible and follow the precepts it sets forth.

What about Prenuptial Agreements?

Prenuptial agreements are legal contracts between two people contemplating marriage. These agreements define what material benefits each spouse will receive if the marriage is dissolved. With divorce becoming an accepted norm in society, such agreements are becoming more common.

The famed Donald and Ivana Trump divorce case focused on the prenuptial arrangements made by the couple before they were married. Although this case was unique, it serves as an illustration of the reality of such a legal arrangement in our culture. The question is, Should a widow consider prenuptial agreements in her remarriage situation?

One reason why a widow might consider a prenuptial agreement is to protect the assets she brings into the second marriage. In commenting on this motive or any other motive for insisting on prenuptial agreements by a widow, Larry Burkett warns that "they drive a wedge in a relationship that will quickly turn into a rift under the right set of conditions."[5]

For a widow to feel she must protect her assets against a future spouse signals a lack of trust on her part. There is a sense in which this legal device can be viewed as programming for failure. The basic love and trust which are fundamental components in any marriage may be threatened by the suggestion of prenuptial agreements.

There may be some allowances for prenuptial agreements in certain circumstances. For example, suppose an older couple marries, and neither has need for the finances of the other. They may agree to have all of their assets held in a trust for the lifetime of either surviving spouse. The couple can draw funds from this trust while they are alive, but when they both die, the heirs are guaranteed the remainder of the assets.

Each situation is different, and widows must seek both spiritual and legal counsel on the matter of entering into prenuptial agreements. Based on his experience in counseling several couples who had prenuptial agreements, Burkett observes that "none of them were benefited by the agreement and most were divided by it."[6]

Summary

Widows may have the need to remarry at some time in their future, but they must not rush into relationships they may well regret later. Widows must heed the words found in Jeremiah 49:11: "Your widows too can trust in me." The Lord will provide the "right one" for the widow.

Care givers can assist the widow not by playing Cupid but by directing her to the scriptural principles related to remarriage and spiritual discernment. Those who have a close relationship with a widow thinking about marriage can ask her the hard questions she needs to answer for herself about remarriage and her selection.

The Lord knows that the missing ingredient in a widow's life is a marriage partner. A new mate will not necessarily solve all of her woes, but he will provide the intimate companionship many widows need. For this reason, the Lord actually encourages widows to remarry.

Questions for Discussion

1. Why does Paul seem to contradict himself in 1 Timothy 5:11, where he speaks negatively about widows who desire to marry, and in verse 14, where he encourages widows to remarry?

2. What are some possible reasons why widowers are not included in the biblical teachings of widowhood?

3. Why does Paul feel that a widow would be happier if she remains single (1 Cor. 7:8, 40)?

4. What are some observable marks of a man who truly belongs to the Lord (1 Cor. 7:39)?

5. What are some of the dangers of entering into

prenuptial agreements? How has divorce in our culture affected prenuptial agreements?

Application

1. Interview a widow who has remarried. Ask her about her challenges, frustrations, and ways of adjusting in her second marriage. What advice would she offer to a widow considering remarriage?

2. Interview a child or children who were blended in a second marriage. How did they accept a new father or mother? How did they accept new siblings? What would they suggest to other children of blended families to cope with their situations?

3. As a pastor or counselor, develop a separate premarital course designed especially for second marriages.

4. List the advantages and disadvantages of prenuptial agreements.

8 *Setting Your House in Order*

꡴

THE PROPHET Isaiah issued a very stunning an-
nouncement to King Hezekiah by saying, "This is what
the LORD says: put your house in order, because you will
die; you will not recover" (2 Kings 20:1). Most husbands,
in contrast to Hezekiah, do not receive advanced knowledge of their death and then set their houses in order, or
make preparations to die. Since death strikes individuals
regardless of their age or status in life, and men statistically die before women, it is critical for husbands to seriously prepare their wives for their inevitable destiny of
widowhood.

The most distressing aspect of widowhood, women
say, is that no one can prepare for it. Women rehearse for
marriage but not for widowhood. The wedding vows
warn the participants there will be a time of separation,
but those words are seldom heard. When death does part
the couple, it seems imaginary. The unfamiliarity evokes
fear and bewilderment, especially in the beginning.

This chapter is a call for husbands who truly care for
their wives to set their houses in order before their de-

parture from this life. By taking a few simple actions, husbands can ease some of the pressures which naturally befall their wives in widowhood. Since 85 percent of married women in America will be widowed in their lifetime and will remain widows for an average of eighteen years, the importance of advance preparation is apparent.[1]

Where There Is a Will There Is Hope

Half the people in the United States who die leave no wills. State law determines how their possessions are to be parceled out.[2] It is fair to say that the average husband does not feel a will is all that important. Sylvia Porter reports that only three out of ten men have an up-to-date will.[3]

I must confess that during the first few years of my own marriage I had not thought seriously about drafting a personal will. Younger husbands feel they really do not have any assets to justify the expense of writing a will. When children came into our family, I realized that they were the greatest assets I possessed. If something happened where both my wife and I died, our children's future would be decided by the courts of our land because of the absence of a will.

A will is a legal document devised to express postmortem objectives. With a will a husband can provide for the welfare of his family, distribute his assets as he thinks best, and secure a responsible person to administrate his estate.

The person designated to administrate the will after the husband dies is called an executor. In most cases the wife is named the executor (referred to as the executrix). If the husband dies without a will, the opportunity to designate an executor is relinquished, thereby leaving open the possibility that someone the husband or wife might not want to manage the estate will be appointed by the probate court.

Some couples assume that the wife automatically inherits all of her husband's property even if there is no will. In some states this assumption is true only in the case of married persons having no children. Where children are involved, the surviving spouse gets one-half of the property, and the children equally share in the other half. The laws regarding matters of death and inheritance differ in each state. A will can address many of these laws and reduce potential material losses for the widow.

Wills may be updated, altered, and revised when necessary. After a husband dies and transfers his assets to his wife through a will, the widow will then have an estate. Subsequently, she will need to revise her will as a widow.

A will does not have to be costly. If most of the information is recorded before a visit to an attorney, the cost can be cut considerably. A confidential data form is contained in appendix C listing the basic information required in writing a will. Once a couple completes this information, they can schedule an appointment with an attorney to write a formal will. The will may cost from two hundred to five hundred dollars depending on the time required by an attorney to complete the work. Opportunities to save taxes by means of well-drawn wills may more than offset the initial cost of a will.

Although a will is fundamental to maintaining individual control over the distribution of assets and the naming of an executor, another option is available in estate planning.

The Living Trust

My father-in-law decided to transfer his property out of his ownership while he was still alive. He remains in control of his property, continues to benefit from his holdings, and may change his beneficiaries and other aspects of his trust. A trust is similar to a will in that both are vehicles by which people may write instructions which allow them to give what they have to whom they want, how and when they want. It differs from a will in that a trust allows a person to transfer his property out of his ownership while he is still alive.

A trust is not the only vehicle in which to save on paying taxes, but there are tax advantages by using a trust with taxable estates over $600,000. An additional advantage of a living trust is found when the husband becomes sick, injured, or disabled. A will goes into force only when death occurs, but a trust can be activated when the provider is mentally incapacitated.

A living trust is more complex and requires more professional services, making it more costly than a will. Regardless of one's preference of leaving a will or a trust, the important point is to prepare one or the other for the sake of the widow. To neglect either of these legal tools reveals an insensitivity on the part of a husband toward his wife when she will be called on to face widowhood. A widow may not rehearse for widowhood, but if her husband has set his house in order, she will be relieved of much stress at a very painful time for her. A loving husband will prepare a will or a trust for his wife before he dies.

Wives also need to take an active part in this preparatory time. Not only do they need to encourage their husbands to write a last will and testament, but they also need to know what is in the will. My wife's grandmother remarried after being widowed in her younger years. Grandma brought a significant estate into her second marriage. Her second husband drafted a will, but she did not realize that he had bequeathed most of her assets to his children from a previous marriage.

Procrastination and indifference are the two greatest enemies of making a will. Regardless of the size of an estate, the making of a will is a wise and considerate step for any husband to take in preparing his wife for widowhood. Such a step will prepare her for the process of probate.

The Probability of Probate

Originally, probate was established to protect creditors by assuring that debts were paid before an estate was divided among the heirs. Today the emphasis is more on providing an orderly way of distributing an estate. Probate is a procedure by which the court determines who gets the property that was owned by the deceased.

Wives should have a general understanding of the probate process before they are widowed. Probate procedures and laws differ from state to state.

The process begins while a widow is still dealing with her grief. It is unfortunate that the laws do not consider the feelings and hurt of the widows. Widows are called on immediately to gather data, conduct a household inventory, and meet with professionals.

Counselors advise widows not to make any decisions during the first year of their widowhood; yet, the probate laws force widows to make instantaneous decisions. However, this is the way it is, and women need to understand the process.

The complexity of probate procedures will be determined by the size of the estate, the claims against it, and the state in which it is administered. Most probates are serviced by attorneys. The will of the deceased is admitted to probate court, and the executor or administrator of the will is appointed.

Next, the widow is required to inventory and value her husband's assets such as guns, furnishings, computer, etc. A special account is opened to deposit estate money to pay debts claimed against the deceased's holdings. Another significant part of this process is the determination of the estate and inheritance tax liability.

The estate of the deceased is viewed as a taxpaying entity by the government. For this reason, a final personal income tax return for the person who died must be filed, and the income tax on the estate (fiduciary tax) is also determined. The final stage of the process is the distribution of the estate in accordance with the will, or to the heirs if the person died without a will.

Since creditors generally have from three to six months to make any claims against the holdings, the estate will remain open at least that long. I have personally worked with widows who have had to endure the probate process for over a year. This does not mean that everything is frozen for a widow. She can still conduct business, pay bills, and receive her insurance benefits while the probate process is in force. If widows understand the length and requirements of this process, they may be better able to cope throughout the ordeal.

If a husband and wife are aware of the probate process, they can make additional preparation by placing many of their assets in joint tenancy with right of survivorship. This simply means that the wife shares in the ownership of her husband's assets. These assets would include a home, automobiles, property, etc. Assets which are held jointly avoid probate, because the deceased was not the sole owner. Other items that are exempt from the probate process include insurance proceeds, retirement benefits to a named beneficiary, and property in a living trust.

Is Life Insurance a Lack of Faith?

A few misguided Christians believe that having insurance is a lack of faith. If insurance of any kind is used to an extreme, it may become a symbol of a lack of faith. "But if used properly—to provide—it is good stewardship," explains Larry Burkett.[4]

One of the most popular ways used today to provide for future supplementary income, especially by those families who are not wealthy in land and investments, is life insurance. Since Social Security payments are made only to the children of a widow, and these payments stop when each child reaches the age of sixteen, it is prudent for the breadwinner to provide supplemental income to support the family after his death.

How much life insurance should a man carry for his family? Burkett offers one simple formula by saying, "The income presently being earned, less the payments no longer required and less the income available, results in the income that needs to be supplied in order for the family to continue living on the same level enjoyed through the income of the husband."[5]

The actual amount of insurance coverage should be based on the insurance money being invested at 10 percent interest. If the additional income need of a widow is $7,000 per year, then a $70,000 policy should be considered by a husband.

Securing adequate life insurance is yet another way in which a husband can set his house in order before he dies. It is a way for him to provide for his relatives, and especially his immediate family (1 Tim. 5:8), after his death.

It Is Appointed Unto Men to Die

Most of us do not like to think about our own mortality. The subject seems to be especially difficult for men. Widows will often observe that couples who were close to them when their husbands were alive have withdrawn from them since their loss. One of the reasons for such withdrawal is that men do not want to be reminded of their own mortality by the life of the widow.

But death is inevitable, and women generally outlive men. These two undeniable facts in life should stimulate men to consider advance planning for death. Husbands can prepare their wives for an easier adjustment to widowhood if they will take some time to plan for the practical details related to their impending deaths.

Funeral Arrangements

A widow is immediately bombarded with a multitude of decisions to make when she receives news of her husband's death. Where should the body be taken? Should an autopsy be authorized? Who should tell the other family members? How should the body be transported? Which funeral home will handle the arrangements? Is he going to be cremated or buried? What kind of a memorial service would her husband prefer? How much is she going to spend on a casket? Is the casket going to be open or closed during the service? Where is he going to be buried? What was his Social Security number? Can she provide the information for the death certificate? How many copies of the death certificate will she require? When will she inform the Social Security office of his death?

Believe it or not, these are only a few of the questions that bewilder a widow in the first days of her widowhood. She will be called on to make critical decisions at a time in her life when she is least capable of coping with such pressure. The funeral director and perhaps a caring pastor will be some of the first in the network of care givers who will assist the widow in the early days. This assistance will be enhanced by the husband who has prepared his funeral arrangements in advance, thus lifting an enormous burden from his wife.

Widows qualify for $250 from Social Security for burial purposes. Since the average charge for a traditional funeral is $4,493, this is only a token payment from the government.[6]

During her seminar on issues of widowhood at Hinson Baptist Church, Doris Sanford asks the husbands who are in attendance to fill out their own death certificates. After they complete this task, Sanford asks, "How many of you found this to be a difficult thing to do?" Most of the men raise their hands. Sanford drives home her point by saying, "Think how much harder it will be for your wives to be required to fill out your death certificates when you die."

Husbands may not feel comfortable with filling out their death certificates in advance, but they can do some simple planning for their funerals. It costs nothing to contact a funeral director and discuss prearrangements for a funeral.

Questions related to the obituary, eulogy, survivors, cremation or burial, and actual funeral service can be addressed in prearrangements. When plans are completed, the funeral director will file the form with the given information and provide the husband with as many copies as he requests. Appendix D is a sample of a funeral prearrangement form which might be used in such preparations.

Making one's own funeral arrangements may seem morbid, but someone must eventually do it. This task usually falls on the widow, because prior arrangements were neglected by the husband. Funerals have two aspects—emotional and financial. "Most often the subject is dealt with at an emotionally charged time, which means that the financial aspects take on lesser importance," explain Fisher and Lane. "This situation is tailor-made for those funeral directors whose sole interest is making money, rather than carrying out the wishes of you and your deceased husband."[7]

The funeral is a cultural process of closure. It is the celebration of a life now ended, an expression of the continuation of human existence, and a release for the family and friends so that they may go forward with their own lives. The funeral process is a necessary one for the widow to successfully cope with her grief. By a husband prearranging his own funeral, he will actually provide his wife with a healing process to manage her future grief much more effectively.

What Should Be Done with His Body?

It is not the purpose of this section to debate the issue of burial versus cremation. Husbands should indicate exactly what they want done with their bodies after they die. If they prefer cremation, they need to communicate what they want done with their ashes. A local funeral director told me not long ago that he has hundreds of individuals' ashes stored in the basement of his funeral home simply because family members do not know what to do with the remains of their loved ones. He is encouraging families to at least bury the ashes in a cemetery.

Some men have found it advantageous to purchase a burial plot in advance. This step not only relieves the prospective widow of one more decision during her grief; it can actually save money to buy now when lots are probably less expensive than later on.

The disadvantage of securing a burial plot is the uncertainty of whether or not the individual will be in the same area when he dies. Those who are transferred because of employment or military assignments may die in another part of the country. This situation would increase costs because of transporting the body back to where the plot is located. In many cemeteries, however, there is the option to sell the lot back for the price of the original cost.

Summary

The suggestion throughout this chapter has been for husbands to take the time to sit down and write out the necessary information which will be required after they die. Rather than place their wives in this extremely difficult position to guess what should be done, husbands can set their houses in order by making these preparations.

Writing a legal will is one of the basic ways a husband can begin to set his house in order. Providing adequate income to replace what will be lost when a husband is gone may be done through life insurance. Taking an inventory of personal possessions and making a written list for future probate purposes are other practical preparations to be considered.

Finally, a husband can prepare his wife for widowhood by prearranging his funeral. The actual service details, the expenses, and the disposing of his remains can all be determined by a husband while he is alive.

Admittedly, the task of preparing one's wife for widowhood through effective estate planning and prearrangements for death is not pleasant. However, each husband must be sensitive to the fact that it will be traumatic for his wife to make the innumerable decisions that will face her during her time of grief. A husband has the golden opportunity while he lives to contribute his support and care of his own wife before she enters widowhood.

Questions for Discussion

1. Why do so few married men have wills or trusts? What are some of the reasons for an indifference toward making a will? Why do so many people procrastinate in writing a will?

2. How could owning life insurance be viewed as a lack of faith? Why could life insurance be a reasonable way to make proper provision for a widow and her family?

3. What is your understanding of the probate process?

4. What are the advantages of prearranging one's own funeral? What are the disadvantages? How would such prearrangements assist a widow in her grief?

5. What are the advantages and disadvantages of burial versus cremation?

Application

1. Plan a one-day seminar in your church to instruct the congregation about issues of death and dying. Provide forms for people to begin making their wills, planning for their funerals, or other matters that would benefit them in the future.

2. Invite an insurance agent in for a class on life insurance to tell about types of insurance, amount of coverage recommended, how to file for benefits, tax implications on policies, etc.

3. Have someone do research and report to the class on the probate laws and process in your state. Role play the actual process, from a widow meeting an attorney for the first time to the close of the probate process.

4. Arrange for your adult Sunday school class or other ministries of the church to visit a local funeral home. Have a working session where each member writes out his or her own funeral service.

5. Organize a debate on the subject of burial versus cremation.

9 Finding Help

ès

Where can we direct widows to find financial, mutual, and resource support? We have already noted the value of networking widows with professionals for certain types of counsel, but are there organizations which exist primarily to help widows in their plight? The widow's might—her strength—will be developed only when there are adequate resources and support for her. The responsibility of care givers is to identify these resources and direct widows to them.

Unfortunately, churches offer very little by way of resources and support for widows. The secular community offers a little more, but overall there is not much help available to widows. This chapter identifies a few of the limited resources and support systems presently available to assist widows.

Check with Caesar

It is not wrong for widows to apply for the government benefits available to them in their plight. Romans 13:4 tells us that government servants are appointed by God "to do you good." A significant portion of our taxes to the government is credited to many of the social programs that provide financial assistance to the needy.

A problem arises when Christians completely transfer their responsibility to care for widows to the government. Three federal support systems in our country may assist widows.

Social Security

One of the most common financial resources available to many widows in our society is Social Security. It is a federal government program designed to replace part of a person's income which has been lost through retirement, disability, or death.

Social Security is like a pipeline, where money collected from today's workers flows into one end of the pipeline and comes out the other end in the form of benefits for today's beneficiaries. The Social Security Administration publishes booklets and forms whereby a person can obtain information about survivors' insurance, Medicare, statement of earnings on which one has paid Social Security, and requests for a Social Security number or replacement card.

For a widow to begin receiving payments from this resource, she will need to contact the nearest Social Security office to make application. A recent law requires all minor children to have a Social Security number to receive benefits. I often accompany or encourage a family member to accompany a widow to the Social Security office within a week after the funeral to start the process, since it usually takes thirty to sixty days before her first payment arrives.

The Social Security Administration has over 1,300 offices conveniently located throughout the country. Representatives from these offices also make regular visits to the neighboring communities. These offices can be found

by consulting a local telephone directory under Social Security Administration or U.S. Government.

Supplemental Security Income

Supplemental Security Income (SSI) is a federal program operated by the Social Security Administration, but
the money to pay SSI benefits comes from income taxes,
not Social Security taxes. People who qualify for SSI
checks include the aged, disabled, or blind, all of whom
do not own much or have much income.

Some widows who have no children and are too
young to qualify for Social Security may actually qualify
for SSI assistance. A widow in this situation may be blind
or disabled, which would allow her to receive payments.

SSI assistance is packaged in different forms. Monthly
checks are the most common form, but this program also
provides other social services such as housekeeping aid,
arrangements for meals, and help with transportation.
The primary advantage of SSI is that it may be the only
option for a widow if she does not qualify immediately
for Social Security.

Military Benefits

Spike retired from the Army, received a monthly retirement check, and enjoyed the privileges of Malmstrom
Air Force Base such as medical and dental services, shopping, and other amenities. When he died, his widow continued to receive both the monthly check and to enjoy
base privileges. This was especially helpful to Delores,
since she was too young to receive any Social Security
benefits.

Three support societies have been established specifically for widows of military veterans. Each is briefly described here.

National Association of Military Widows

The goal of the National Association of Military Widows is to assure fair treatment of all military widows by using legislation, networking, publication, mutual support, and economic means to accomplish its goal.[1]

The group cooperates with the Veterans Administration, the Department of Defense, and other federal agencies to provide resources for widows. A newsletter is published to communicate to military widows the changes in military health insurance coverage (CHAMPUS), Social Security benefits, and other significant areas.

Society of Military Widows

The Society of Military Widows serves two purposes: (1) to insure that widows' benefits are not cut; and (2) to assist those widows who need help in securing their husbands' military benefits.

Although this group maintains local chapters throughout the United States, it merged with a larger organization called the National Association for Uniformed Services (NAUS).[2] This society may be of limited assistance to military widows.

The Retired Officers Association

Retired military officers from any of the military branches in the United States may join the Retired Officers Association. One of this organization's most helpful resources for widows is the publication *Help Your Widow While She's Still Your Wife*. This fifty-page guide is filled with information concerning federal government regulations on various military payments and benefits available to widows, burial eligibility for national cemeteries, and sample forms to take care of personal affairs in the event of widowhood.[3]

This attractive booklet should be secured and consulted by anyone who may be assisting military widows. If there is a military community near your church, the church should have a copy for reference purposes. Officers who are either retired from military service or continue to actively serve in the military should obtain a copy of this publication and use it to prepare their wives for widowhood. The section entitled "Personal Affairs Workbook" is an extremely valuable portion of the booklet.

Government resources have often been criticized and misunderstood, but when a widow needs extra income subsidy, Social Security, SSI, and military benefits are some of the ways the Lord has allowed widows to receive financial strength.

Find Like Kind

Government sources meet some of the financial needs widows face, but widows require support in other areas as well. The best one to help a widow with her reentry into society as a single person is another widow. A widow who has already successfully handled her own grief saves indispensable time for the development of a contemporary mutual help group.

The first thing that becomes evident to a new widow is the fact that she lives in a couples-oriented society. One widow observed that most banquets, parties, and other social gatherings arrange chairs around tables in sets of twos, fours, or other even numbers. Widows quickly get the message that the social event is arranged with couples in mind.

The new life of singleness for many widows creates social fears that cause them to react in strange ways. A few groups exist that target widows to help them reenter society in a healthy manner.

Widowed Persons Service

Terri Speicher, a widow in Dallas, found a way to help widows through a secular organization, the Widowed Persons Service. "I heard about it after being widowed over two years," she says. "At that point I was ready to pass on some of the comfort I had received and began by taking their volunteer training seminar."

Speicher says she is frequently able to add a spiritual dimension to group meetings. "I have used this group to meet both believing and nonbelieving widowed persons. I usually have Christian speakers and witness freely in one-on-one situations."

There are five components to the Widowed Persons Service.[4] The outreach component consists of widowed volunteers who visit the newly bereaved and discuss on a one-on-one basis their adjustments to the problems of widowhood.

The telephone service is the component in which widows may call for referral or assistance information. The group sessions are a component that brings the widowed together to discuss mutual problems and possible solutions.

Public education, another component of the organization, uses the resources of local public service agencies and educational media to call attention to the needs of the widowed and services available to them. A published

list of films, videocassettes, filmstrips, and slide presenta-
tions related to widowhood is available on request.

The final component consists of a referral system. This
system is contained in a directory or manual of local services that may be of assistance to widows.

A wealth of opportunities for involvement is available
to widows through the Widowed Persons Service. Those
who have been widowed eighteen months or longer are
eligible to train for reach-out activities to the newly widowed in the community. Other volunteers, widowed and
nonwidowed, may contribute their skills by fund-raising,
board participation, and administrative duties.

To Live Again

Catherine Marshall, a widow, wrote about her own
widowhood in a book titled *To Live Again*. The title of this
book was eventually used by five recently widowed persons to name a new organization for widows.

In 1973 the organization held its first To Live Again
conference in Philadelphia. This conference was designed to address the financial, legal, spiritual, and emotional needs of the newly widowed. The success of this
conference led to the birth and growth of a national organization that seeks to help widows "to live again."

To Live Again (TLA), like Weight Watchers and other
mutual support groups, has local chapters which hold
regular meetings.[5] TLA members host these meetings at
churches, senior citizen centers, professional buildings,
and community centers.

One of the highlights of TLA is their semiannual conference where widows enjoy practical workshops, a
keynote speaker, delicious food, and mutual fellowship.
Several resources are available to widows through this

group. *The Pioneer* (TLA news calendar) lists the local chapters and the calendar of events for the organization.

THEOS

Another widow, Bea Decker, of Penn Hills, Pennsylvania, was frustrated by the lack of any meaningful support system for widows. Her Lutheran denomination provided no formal support for widows, and she was convinced that her denomination promised nothing for widows in the future.

Determined to do something about this lack of support, Decker gained permission from her church to use its building facilities for a support group meeting. "Rev. Gerhard volunteered to write the local press explaining the motives of the new organization," she explains. "On February 25, 1962, less than nine months after Bob's death, more than sixty-five interested persons from Pennsylvania and Ohio attended the first meeting. That was the beginning of a new type of ministry for the widowed."[6]

THEOS is an acronym for They Help Each Other Spiritually.[7] The mission of the organization is to promote healing and wholeness for bereaved women. It is an ecumenical ministry which emphasizes the spiritual needs of widows. The "THEOS Communicator" is a newsletter published six times a year to inform widows of events, workshops, and other programs.

Churches who desire to host a local chapter may write for an organizational kit and make formal application. The organization publishes very practical literature in caring for widows. The *Survivors Outreach* magazine is published eight times a year to offer useful tips related to the subject of widowhood. A THEOS cookbook with single-serving recipes and inspiration, a pamphlet, "What to Say to a Widow," and a THEOS pin are a few of the resources available through this group.

There are other less notable groups where widows can find others experiencing widowhood, but they are few and far between. Some widows may have to consider developing their own support group in their community as Bea Decker did. At least resources can be used from groups like the Widowed Persons Service, TLA, and THEOS so widows do not have to reinvent the organizational wheel of such a support group.

Keep Learning

Many women find themselves as displaced homemakers when they are widowed. A displaced homemaker is an individual who has, for a substantial number of years, provided unpaid service to her family and been dependent on her spouse for her income, but she has lost that income through death, divorce, separation, desertion, or the disablement of her husband. Two-thirds of the 11.5 million displaced homemakers in the United States are widows.[8]

Forty percent of displaced homemakers are living below poverty level.[9] The dilemmas most displaced homemakers face are that they have not acquired many skills that make them gainfully employable, they are often too old for many jobs, and yet they are too young for Social Security and other governmental benefits.

The Displaced Homemakers Network was established in 1974 by a fifty-seven-year-old woman who found herself divorced after twenty-three years as a homemaker, wife, mother, and volunteer community activist. Imme-

diately, Tish Sommers became aware of the problems former dependent homemakers encounter when they lose
their "job."

Sommers set out to help these women survive and
reconstruct independent lives for themselves after the
loss of their spouses. Her motto was, "Organize, don't
agonize."

Through its Washington office, Displaced Homemakers
Network works to increase displaced homemakers' op-
tions for economic self-sufficiency, to provide information
on public policy issues that affect displaced homemakers,
to provide technical assistance resources for service
providers, and to help staff members around the country
locate the information and expertise they need to develop programs for displaced homemakers.[10]

Jobs are the primary need for displaced homemakers.
All of the resources available through this organization
relate to the preparation of women who are forced to en-
ter the work force. Career exploration, job readiness
training, educational assistance, and mutual-help groups
are the four primary services offered by Displaced Homemakers Network.

Women are never too old to learn new skills and employ these skills in the marketplace. Often what is lack-
ing is the knowledge of how to get started. The network
provides the knowledge of how to receive training and
gain employment for those widows who are displaced
homemakers.

Public education and outreach programs directed toward the continuing problems that plague widows are a
few of the resources the network provides. An example
of this is seen in the network's cooperative efforts with the
American Association of Retired Persons to produce
"Partners in Change," an award-winning video that helps

employers understand the benefits of hiring older displaced homemakers.

Summary

Finding help in a time of need is critical for a widow to remain strong. Government agencies offer primarily financial assistance, but such aid alone is insufficient to fully meet the economic essentials of a woman's life. Care givers should be familiar with the specialized support available to widows of military veterans.

Churches should train widows in their own congregations to reach out to new widows and assist them in their time of need. Some of the strongest support will come from widows ministering to other widows. They understand each other, they know how to effectively care, and they receive the satisfying reward of helping others.

A few major organizations specifically deal with issues of widowhood. These groups offer helpful resources and guidance for local ministries to widows. Widows are often the ones who initiate grassroots organizations to meet not only their own needs but also the needs of others.

People in smaller churches can find ways to care for widows even if they lack the resources to develop formal programs. Helen, who lives in a rural area, chauffeurs widows to town for shopping and doctor appointments. One man helped a widow in his church move a boundary fence on her property. There are no limits to the practical ways widows can find help in their distress.

Questions for Discussion

1. Based on Romans 13:1–6, why is it acceptable for widows to receive government aid?

2. Why should we not expect government aid to completely meet the financial needs of a widow?

3. How could a church considering development of a ministry for widows benefit from the secular organizations that are already serving widows? What dimension could the church add to a ministry for widows that other organizations could not offer?

4. Why is one of the most effective care givers to a widow another widow? What would they have in common? What might be some problems in one widow ministering to another widow?

5. Why are the circumstances of a widow who is also a displaced homemaker so difficult? How is this difficulty compounded if she has children at home?

Application

1. Secure your credited earnings for the past ten years from the Social Security Administration.

2. If you are a veteran, find out what benefits your wife will receive upon your death.

3. Write to one of the organizations mentioned in this chapter to request resources they offer for the care of widows.

4. Sponsor one of the widows in your church so she can attend one of the national conferences on widowhood.

5. Investigate a local Displaced Homemakers Network chapter in your area to discover what services are available to the widows in your locality.

10 *Mobilizing the Church*

ໃ**

THIS ENTIRE BOOK is about you and your church making a difference by caring for widows. The information provided throughout these chapters is intended to be more than an academic exercise in research and theory. The outcome of this book should be found in local churches mobilizing their members to develop a systematic, continual, and growing ministry to widows.

An appeal has been made for the church to return to its biblical responsibility to provide the needed strength for the approximately nine million widows in our country.[1] Such a return may occur on a small scale in one local church, but as the testimony of that church's care for widows spreads, other churches will catch the vision and follow the example by developing their own ministries of care for widows.

Monkey See, Monkey Do

I heard a leading educator say that the best method of teaching is still "monkey see, monkey do." Churches can learn how to launch effective ministries to widows by watching what other churches are doing and then following their examples. I would like to present three models where ministries to widows are occurring.

Hinson Memorial Baptist Church

In October 1985, a small band of concerned widows from Hinson Memorial Baptist Church located in Portland, Oregon, submitted a proposal for a widows-helping-widows group to the leaders of the church. The four major points of this proposal reflect the needs to which the widows appealed to this church to respond in a formal way.

The first point was for continuing education in the church to prepare its members for the eventuality of death. The proposal suggested that Doris Sanford, a widow and instructor of thanatology at Mt. Hood Community College, teach a series of classes on bereavement to the church members.

The second point of the proposal encouraged widows to join a widows-helping-widows group. This group was structured so widows would not become dependent on it long-term. It emphasized the nurturing of new leaders and encouraged widows to reach out to other widows in ministry. Special speakers were invited to address topics of real concern to widows.

The third part of the proposal was to have Hinson follow the lead of the early church (Acts 6) and designate a deacon or someone else to look after the needs of each widow. The appointment of a deacon and his wife from the church to visit a new widow monthly for the first two years of her new life was suggested.

The final point of this proposal was to provide each widow with a list of names, addresses, and phone numbers of persons and agencies in her community to whom she could go for help. This recommendation networked other helping agencies with the widows' ministry of the local church.

The leaders of the church approved the proposal in 1986, and several committed women went to work to mobilize a viable widows' support group.

An annual grief workshop was established at Hinson for widows, members of the church, and the general population throughout the greater Portland area. Monthly meetings are conducted on Sunday afternoons at the church.

After a widow has been in the care group for two years, she graduates out of the ministry as she has known it. The graduating widow is taken to lunch by a widow-to-widow coordinator and given an opportunity to evaluate her adjustment to widowhood.

Once a widow has completed two years as a participant in the ministry, she may advance to a new role as a leader or care giver to help with new widows in the group. Judith Stewart, president of Hinson's widow-to-widow ministry, explains, "We do not want widows to become dependent indefinitely on a support group. There comes a time when each widow must get on with her life."

This local church ministry to widows meets a definite need in this neglected area of church care. Many commendable features of this ministry can be reproduced.

First Evangelical Free Church

The First Evangelical Free Church of Fullerton, California, is pastored by Charles Swindoll. This local church organized a widows' group nine years ago under the capable leadership of Betty Coble Lawther, director of women's ministries.

The mutual care groups for widows in this church meet weekly from 7:30 to 9:30 A.M. During the first half-hour the women meet informally for refreshments. The next ten minutes are used to communicate information about how grief is expressed. The remainder of the time is spent in small groups of eight to ten widows with a group leader who has been through the group and feels ready to meet with newly grieved people.

New groups are initiated when an established group grows beyond ten to twelve widows. The new members of a group are people who have been widowed for one week to one year depending on when they hear about the group or when they get enough courage to attend.

The ministry sponsors a variety of social events for widows. Once a month they gather for a potluck dinner. Another monthly social may be a "group date" where the widows attend a dinner theater or go on a local trip.

The primary objective of this widows' ministry is to help widows complete a fifty-two-week course on every aspect of grief. The ultimate goal is to help each widow talk through and think through her loss and begin to make new memories and form new directions.

Emmanuel Bible Church

Located on the east slopes of the Rocky Mountains in Great Falls, Montana, is the Emmanuel Bible Church. I have served as its pastor for fifteen years. Although I have studied the subject of widowhood for the greater part of these years, it was not until November 1991 that a ministry to widows was established at the church.

The ministry is called the Widow's Might Ministry. Its

mission statement is that the church is to be biblically proactive as a community of believers in taking care of the widows in the church, community, and region. Our aim is to prepare families for eventual widowhood, provide for the individual needs of widows, and protect widows in their vulnerable state. Appendix E is a flow chart to illustrate how the parts of the widows' ministry fit together.

The widows meet on the last Sunday of each month at the church from 3:00 to 5:00 P.M. The two-hour sessions are divided by using the first thirty minutes for a Bible study on a particular area of widowhood. In the next half-hour segment the widows participate in small-group discussions. A guest speaker, video, panel discussion, or other special features are scheduled for the following portion of the meeting. Finally, the last part of the meeting is a fellowship time for the widows to enjoy refreshments and one another.

These meetings are advertised throughout the region. Community service announcements are aired over the Christian radio station, advertisements are placed in the local newspaper, and the widows themselves invite others to attend the meetings. Once the news of these meetings has circulated throughout the region, women from both the city and the county will often call the church office to inquire about the widows' ministry.

There has been an overwhelming reception to this ministry for widows. One widow who attends another church in the area has been asked by her pastor to conduct a seminar on widowhood for the women of her church. The enthusiasm and concern to reach out in caring for the widows of our community is spreading like a prairie fire. The flames of caring for widows can spread in your area as you mobilize your church to begin a ministry of care for widows.

The widows have several projects they would like to accomplish over the next several months. One is the development of a "Widows' Yellow Pages," which would list information about reputable services in the community for widows to consult. Another project, which will require additional time, is to lobby for property tax relief for those widows who own their homes. Often a widow is left with a home to live in but is unable to afford to pay the high property taxes. The state of Florida grants widows an automatic $500 relief from their property taxes. This relief is significant because a large population of older Americans forms an enormous tax base in that state.

The three churches presented as models for widows' ministries may differ as to exact program emphases, schedules, and approaches, but the common threads of preparing, providing, and protecting widows in their plight will be found in each of these ministries. Churches can learn from others how to provide the essential care required by their widows.

It Begins at the Top

For any ministry to widows to be a success, it is vital for the leaders of the local church not only to vocalize their support but also to become actively involved. This is not to say that the pastor solely should be responsible for the care of widows in the church. Other leaders in the church such as the elders, deacons, and deaconesses should be encouraged to develop a ministry to widows within the life of the church.

At Hinson the pastor begins the care process by making an immediate call on a new widow and leaving her a book by Doug Manning, *Don't Take My Grief Away*. Next, a letter is sent from the church to invite the widow to the next monthly widow-to-widow meeting.

Occasionally, I conduct an in-service workshop with my elders and deacons. The Southern Baptist Convention produced a video series titled "Caring Roles of Deacons," which became an effective educational tool for my own leaders.

If our church leaders do not exhibit care for widows, then the church as a whole will not care. A widow consciousness must be developed as a corporate image throughout the church. This image begins at the top and filters down to the laypersons of the church.

At times we have assigned the care of individual widows to either the leaders of the church, other laypersons, or both. Each man and wife visit their assigned widow, monitor her needs, and assist her in meeting those needs throughout the year.

The Widows' Fund

At the biannual meeting in June 1991 at Emmanuel Bible Church, I submitted a proposal to establish a special widows' fund. Our church already had a benevolent fund that provides for the needy, but this fund was to serve a different purpose.

One of the aims of the widows' ministry is to provide for the individual needs of widows. The formulation of a special widows' fund was one practical way to reach the objective of assisting widows financially. Since the church is responsible for the support of widows who are destitute of family and finances (1 Tim. 5:3, 5, 9, 16), a distinct fund was initiated solely for the purpose of providing for the needs of such widows in the church.

A plan of action was written to explain to the congregation exactly how this fund would be supplied without its detracting from other giving to the church, how the fund would be administered, and how a widow would apply for the needed funds.

This special fund has not been needed at this point, but it is in place, and people in the church are aware they may contribute to the fund at any time. When a widow does have a financial need, the church will be ready to respond to it.

How to Get Started

I have found that the hardest part of jogging is getting out the front door. As the Nike commercial says, "Just do it." A ministry of care for widows through the local church should start small and simply, but it should start.

The first step in mobilizing the church to begin a targeted ministry of care for widows is to convince leaders of the need of such a vital ministry. The leaders, in turn, must teach the church members about the biblical priority of caring for widows. Remember, care for widows must begin at the top and trickle down.

The second step is to write out a plan of action for a ministry to widows. This plan should include a well-written mission statement, goals, objectives, and methods to give direction to the ministry. A careful strategy must be developed to insure a lasting ministry for widows in the church.

The third step is to recruit and train widows in the church to make this ministry their own. They must plan the monthly meetings, serve refreshments, counsel other widows, and provide transportation for widows.

A fourth step is actually to get the widows together for meaningful times. Challenging them to reenter society as whole persons, instructing them about their new roles, and providing opportunities for them to serve will make their times together worthwhile.

A final step is to evaluate the ministry periodically. Is the widows' ministry fulfilling its intended purpose? Are widows excited about what is going on in the church as it relates to them? How can the ministry be improved? What are we doing right? What are we doing wrong? These are just a few questions which should be asked of any ministry.

Summary

In comparison, the secular community is providing more care for widows than the church community. This trend needs to be reversed by churches that mobilize their efforts at caring for widows on a consistent, meaningful basis. A few churches have taken seriously their responsibility to care for widows. These churches may be used as examples for other churches to activate similar care.

The attitude and actions of leaders in the local church are critical for any program of care to be initiated. Care for widows in the early church began with a concern by the apostles and other leaders (Acts 6:1–6). It is no different in this century or in our culture. Care begins at the top.

A systematic approach will assure a functional ministry to widows. It is not as difficult to sponsor a ministry for widows as it is to simply get started on a small scale. The rewards and the satisfaction of "looking after widows in their distress" (James 1:27) make all of the planning and efforts for a ministry to widows worthwhile.

Questions for Discussion

1. What are some lessons your church might learn from the three churches presented in this chapter for establishing a ministry for widows?

2. What are some of the common features in each of the three churches as they relate to the widows' ministries? What are some things that would not work in your situation?

3. How could a widow or someone who is concerned about widows encourage church leaders to get excited about a widows' ministry?

4. How could you as a pastor begin to train your leaders and laypersons to become "widow conscious"?

5. What is preventing your church from establishing a ministry for widows today? When could you realistically begin such a ministry? Could you cooperate with other churches in your area to begin this ministry?

Application

1. Visit a regular meeting of a widows' ministry and observe how the meeting is conducted.

2. Develop a plan of action for a ministry to widows in your church. Target an exact time when you will put this plan into force.

3. Establish a special widows' fund in your church to assist in the financial needs of widows.

4. To evaluate your current ministry to widows, identify strengths and weaknesses in which to make improvements in the ministry.

CONCLUSION

A WOMAN entering widowhood has been compared to a woman finding herself unexpectedly in a foreign country. She does not understand the strange language, she is required to make important decisions in this condition, and she is dependent on interpreters with a poor command of English.

If we can appreciate the fear and bewilderment that such a situation would evoke, then we can begin to imagine what it is like to become a widow in a society characterized by an insensitivity toward her plight. The church must not be characterized by the same insensitivity as the rest of the world. It must return to giving loving care to women who have experienced significant losses.

A few years have passed since Vern's death. Unlike many, Susan did not remain a widow. She began a second marriage and a new life. This does not mean that she has forgotten her painful journey.

Her advice to churches? Widows want to be included in the life of the church, just as they were when their husbands were alive. "Don't treat them any differently," she says. "Widows want understanding, not pity."

NOTES ❧

Introduction

1. Stanley Cornils, "Does Your Church Take Care of Its Widows?" *Christianity Today* (July 15, 1983): 60.

2. Phyllis R. Silverman, "Widowhood and Preventive Intervention," *The Family Coordinator* (January 1972): 95.

3. Ibid.

4. Linda Solie and Lois J. Fielder, "The Relationship Between Sex Role Identity and a Widow's Adjustment to the Loss of a Spouse," *Omega: Journal of Death and Dying* 18 (1987–88): 33.

Chapter 1

1. Charles F. Fensham, "Widow, Orphan, and the Poor in Ancient Near Eastern Legal and Wisdom Literature," *Journal of Near Eastern Studies,* 21 (April 1973): 129.

2. P. C. Craige, *The Book of Deuteronomy, The New International Commentary on the Old Testament* (Grand Rapids: Wm. B. Eerdmans Publishing Company, 1976), 308.

3. Ronald de Vaux, *Ancient Israel: Its Life and Institutions,* trans. John McHugh (New York: McGraw-Hill Book Company, Inc., 1961), 21.

4. Alfred Allan Lewis and Barrie Berns, *Three Out of Four Wives* (New York: Macmillan Publishing Co., Inc., 1975), 97.

5. J. Oswald Sanders, *The Incomparable Christ* (Chicago: Moody Press, 1952), 165.

6. Gustiv Stahlin, "Χήρα," in *Theological Dictionary of the New Testament,* ed. Gerhard Kittel (Grand Rapids: Wm. B. Eerdmans, 1975), 9.

Chapter 2

1. Homer Kent, Jr., *The Pastoral Epistles: Studies in I and II Timothy and Titus* (Chicago: Moody Press, 1958), 171.

2. H. Wayne House, "Distinctive Roles of Women in the Second and Third Centuries," *Bibliotheca Sacra,* 146 (January 1989): 41. Dr. Kent in *The Pastoral Epistles: Studies in I and II Timothy and Titus,* p. 172, and Dr. Charles Ryrie in *The Role of Women in the Church,* p. 82, share this view.

3. Patrick Fairbairn, *Pastoral Epistles* (T & T Clark, 1974; reprint, Minneapolis: James & Klock Publishing Co., 1976). Fairbairn provides a very helpful survey of the differing schools of thought on this passage (see pp. 198–201).

4. Adele Rice Nudel, *Starting Over: Help for Young Widows and Widowers* (New York: Dodd, Mead & Co., 1986), 6.

5. Ibid.

Chapter 3

1. Phyllis Silverman and Adele Cooperband, "Widow-to-Widow: The Elderly Widow and Mutual Help," in *The World of the Older Woman,* vol. III, Frontiers in Aging Series, ed. Gari Lesnoff-Caravaglia (New York: Human Sciences Press, 1984), 147.

Chapter 4

1. Philomene Gates, *Suddenly Alone: A Woman's Guide to Widowhood* (New York: Harper & Row, Publishers, 1990), 3.

2. Lynn Caine, *Being a Widow* (New York: Arbor House, 1988), 20.

3. Beverley Raphael, *The Anatomy of Bereavement* (New York: Basic Books, 1983), 213–14.

4. Caine, p. 23.

5. Ruby Banks Abrahams, "Mutual Help for the Widowed," *Social Work* 17 (Sept. 1972): 54.

6. Howard Clinebell, *Basic Types of Pastoral Care & Counseling* (Nashville: Abingdon Press, 1984), 218.

7. The International Lay Pastoral Care Ministry can be contacted at: Hope Presbyterian Church, 7132 Portland Ave. So., Richfield, MN 55423. A quarterly newsletter may be received on request.

8. Warren W. Wiersbe and David W. Wiersbe, *Comforting the Bereaved* (Chicago: Moody Press, 1985), 25.

Chapter 5

1. D. R. Jones and P. O. Goldblatt, "Causes of Death in Widow(er)s and Spouses," *Journal of Biosocial Science* 19 (1987): 108.
2. Ibid.
3. David Maddison and Agnes Viola, "The Health of Widows in the Year Following Bereavement," *Journal of Psychosomatic Research* 12 (July 1968): 304.
4. Ibid.
5. Donald C. Cushenbery and Rita Crossley Cushenbery, *Coping with Life After Your Mate Dies* (Grand Rapids: Baker Book House, 1991), 33.
6. Gates, p. 29.

Chapter 6

1. Lewis and Berns, p. 97.
2. Anne McGrath, Maureen Walsh, Nancy Linnon, and Sharon Golden, "Living Alone and Loving It," *U.S. News and World Report* (August 1987): 54.
3. Caine, p. 201.
4. Anna M. Brock, "From Wife to Widow," *Journal of Gerontological Nursing* 10 (April 1984): 8.
5. Larry Burkett, *The Complete Financial Guide for Single Parents* (Wheaton: Victor Books, 1991), 134.
6. Malcolm Carter, "Saving Widows from Still More Losses," *Money* (May 1981): 90.
7. Ibid.
8. Burkett, p. 125.
9. Gates, p. 69. This author provides very helpful material on exactly what to look for in hiring an attorney.

Chapter 7

1. *NCCI Remarriage Tables*, "Exhibit IV-B: Select Absolute Rates of Remarriage," (1975): 94.
2. Burkett, p. 150.

3. Miriam Baker Nye, *But I Never Thought He'd Die* (Philadelphia: The Westminster Press, 1978), 136.

4. Ibid., p. 137.

5. Burkett, p. 150.

6. Ibid.

Chapter 8

1. Abrahams, p. 54.

2. Laura Lane, "Spendthrifty: Your Principal Heir Could Be Uncle Sam," *CGA World* 3 (May/June 1983): 5.

3. Cornils, p. 60.

4. Burkett, p. 134.

5. Ibid., p. 198.

6. United Communications Group, *Funeral Service Insider* 17 (Oct. 12, 1992): 2.

7. Ida Fisher and Byron Lane, *The Widow's Guide to Life,* (Englewood Cliffs: Prentice-Hall, Inc., 1981), 15.

Chapter 9

1. Jean Arthurs, chairperson of the National Association of Military Widows may be contacted by writing to the national office: 4023 - 25th Road North, Arlington, VA 22207.

2. Della Moore, "SMW: A Helping Hand for Military Widows," *Uniformed Services Journal* (May–June, 1988): 13–14.

3. Edward S. Gryczynski, Lewis J. Tolleson, and Elizabeth H. Audie, *Help Your Widow While She's Still Your Wife,* (Alexandria: The Retired Officers Association, 1988). This valuable publication may be obtained by writing to the association's address: 201 N. Washington St., Alexandria, VA 22314-2529.

4. The national address for the Widowed Persons Service is: 1909 K Street, N.W., Washington, D.C. 20049.

5. The address and phone number for To Live Again Central is Post Office Box 415, Springfield, PA 19064-0415. Telephone: 215-353-7740.

6. Beatrice Decker, *After the Flowers Have Gone* (Grand Rapids: Zondervan Publishing House, 1973), 31. This book is the author's personal story of the birth of THEOS.

7. International THEOS Foundation, 1301 Clark Building, 717 Liberty Avenue, Pittsburgh, PA 15222.

8. U.S. Bureau of Census, *Current Population Reports: Supplement Report, 1986,* series p. 23 no. 152.

9. Ibid.

10. Displaced Homemakers Network is located at 1411 K Street, N.W., Suite 930, Washington, D.C. 20005.

Chapter 10

1. Felix M. Berardo, "Widowed Status in the United States: Perspective on a Neglected Aspect of the Family Life-Cycle," *The Family Coordinator* 17 (July 1968): 191. This is a conservative figure as later material estimates closer to 10 million widows. Peter T. Chew, "Ten Million Widows: Few Are Merry," *National Observer* (Aug. 4, 1973): 1.

Appendix A
Widows Visitation Report

Your Name _____ Month _____

Widow's Name _____ Date Visited _____

Length of Visit _____

AREA OF NEED	STATED NEED	HOW NEED WAS/WILL BE MET

Personal

How has the past month been for you?

How do you spend most of the day? Evening?

What had your husband always done that you don't feel comfortable doing?

Are you feeling well? Able to cook? Eat?

Are you comfortable with the amount of time you are with friends?

Is there a male role model for your children?

How are your children handling their grief?

Do you need child care?

Help with correspondence?

Other?

Practical

What is broken or not working in the house?

Do you need help with yard maintenance? Pruning? Hauling to dump? Gutters cleaned? Hoses brought in? Is antifreeze in?

How is your car working? Last serviced?

Do you have any transportation needs?

Christmas tree delivery and setup?

Help with house plants?

Other?

Financial

Have you applied for life insurance benefits?

Do you have enough money to live on now? Or to tide you over?

Are you going to need help finding employment?

What are your long-term income plans?

Is your will rewritten?

Do you need legal counsel?

Do you need financial counsel?

Appendix B
Preparing . . .
Just in Case

ESTATE PLANNING material is available from the book *Preparing . . . Just in Case* by Patricia A. Frishkoff and Bonnie M. Brown. It invites you to provide your family with certain information needed in case of sudden illness, death, or other catastrophe. All people who genuinely care about their families can take this workbook and plan their futures around sharing, preparedness, and dignity. The *Preparing . . . Just in Case* workbook and other material may be obtained by sending your name and address with a check for $19.95 plus $3.00 shipping payable to OSU Family Business Program at the following address:

Family Business Program
College of Business, Bexell Hall 201
Oregon State University
Corvallis, OR 97331-2603
Phone (503) 737-3326, FAX (503)737-4890

Appendix C
Confidential Data Form

General Information

Date _____

Family Information

	Age	Marital Status	Health Status
Name _____	__	_____	_____
Spouse _____	__	_____	_____

Address _____

City_____ State _____ Zip _____

Telephone _____ Township _____ County _____

Children

Name	Age	Marital Status	Health Status	Name of Spouse
_____	__	_____	_____	_____
_____	__	_____	_____	_____
_____	__	_____	_____	_____
_____	__	_____	_____	_____
_____	__	_____	_____	_____

Other Dependents

_____	__	_____	_____	_____
_____	__	_____	_____	_____
_____	__	_____	_____	_____

Employment

Your Employer_____ Occupation _____

Spouse's Employer _____ Occupation _____

Business Address _____ Telephone _____

Social Security Number_____ Spouse's Social Security Number _____

117

Estate Information

Real Estate	**Ownership**		
	Yours	Spouse's	Joint
1. Residence			
Market value	$_____	$_____	$_____
Deduct mortgage balance	(_____)	(_____)	(_____)
Equity	_____	_____	_____
2. Other Location			
a. _____ _____	_____	_____	_____
b. _____ _____	_____	_____	_____
c. _____ _____	_____	_____	_____
Personal Property			
1. Stocks (Market Value)	_____	_____	_____
2. Bonds (Market Value)	_____	_____	_____
a. Corporate	_____	_____	_____
b. Government	_____	_____	_____
c. Other	_____	_____	_____
3. Cash Accounts			
a. Checking accounts	_____	_____	_____
b. Savings accounts	_____	_____	_____
c. Other	_____	_____	_____
4. Household Furnishings and Miscellaneous Personal Items	_____	_____	_____
5. Notes Receivable	_____	_____	_____
6. Other Assets	_____	_____	_____
Business Interests (Net Worth)	_____	_____	_____
Life Insurance (Death Value)	_____	_____	_____
Retirement Plans			
1. Personal	_____	_____	_____
2. Company	_____	_____	_____
Prospective Inheritance	_____	_____	_____
TOTALS	_____	_____	_____
Estate Total (Add all joint and individual above)	_____		
Less Debts (Other than residence mortgage)	_____		
TOTAL NET ESTATE	$_____		

Planning Information

A. Present Estate Plan

    1. Do you have a will? _____ Spouse? _____ Approximately how old? _____

    2. Do you have a trust? _____ Spouse? _____ Who is trustee? _____

B. Naming an Executor
    An executor serves as your personal representative after your death to see that the terms of your will are carried out. He (she) should be someone who is capable of taking responsibility and is reasonably familiar with your affairs. Husbands and wives usually serve as executor for each other's estate, but if you have a trust, the trustee usually desires to serve as coexecutor of your estate.

Executor's Name _____Address _____ Relationship_____

Alternate Executor _____Address _____ Relationship_____

C. Naming a Guardian
    If you and your spouse should die leaving minor children, whom would you wish to serve as their guardian? We suggest someone quite familiar to your children, with similar religious beliefs, similar attitudes toward child rearing, and where possible, similar economic status. (Of course, your estate will be available to the guardian for your children's care, support, and education.)

Primary

Name _____Address _____ Relationship_____

Alternate (In case the above at that time is unable to serve)

Name _____Address _____ Relationship_____

D. Age to Inherit
    If, after you and your spouse have both died, you intend to leave your estate (or a portion of it) to your children, what age should each attain before control of that portion of the estate passes to the child?

E. Attorney
    Do you have an attorney you would like to counsel with regarding your estate plan?

Name _____Phone _____

City _____State _____Zip _____

Do you want us to recommend an attorney for this work?_____

Distribution Information

1. If you were to die within the next five years, who are the dependents you would want to receive support from your estate—other than your spouse or minor children?

Name_____Relationship_____Age _____Type of Support _____

Name_____Relationship_____Age _____Type of Support _____

2. Itemize specific articles, e.g. antiques, jewelry, works of art, etc., that you want given to a specific person.

Article (Describe briefly)	Person	City, State

3. After you and your spouse have both died and the support needs indicated in item 1 above have been cared for, how would you want the remainder of your estate divided and distributed? At this point, assuming all your children are of legal age and their education needs have been provided for, the estate is then ready for final distribution. It is at this point that lump sums will be given to your children and distributions made to the Lord's work or others.

Name of person or organization	Address	Percentage
1.		_____%
2.		_____%
3.		_____%
4.		_____%
5.		_____%
6.		_____%
7.		_____%
TOTAL (Be sure the percentages add up to 100%)		_____%

A clause should be added to your will to insure orderly distribution in the event any named beneficiary of your will or trust should die before that share is to be received. Many desire that unless the predeceased beneficiary has children, his portion is divided among the remaining beneficiaries, proportionate to the share that he received of the whole.

Does this reflect your thinking and desire? _____

If not, how would you want this handled? _____

_____

Appendix D
Funeral Service
Information

Cemetery or Mausoleum _____

Are Facilities Reserved?   Yes ☐   No ☐

Lot No. _____ Block or Section_____ Grave No. _____

Church Denomination _____

Clergyman _____

Place of Service   Church ☐   Mortuary ☐

Lodge or Organization Participation   Yes ☐   No ☐

_____

Favorite Hymns or Organ Selections:

_____

_____

Other Information:

_____

_____

_____

Vital Statistics and Biographical Record

This form is prepared primarily for use in conjunction with the arrangement or prearrangement of funeral services.

The information requested in the vital statistics section is very important, since legal documents are prepared from this information, and should be exact and correct.

We also recommend that a recent picture be made available for the paper, if this is desired, or to assist us with such details as hairstyling.

Full Name

First _____ Middle _____ Last _____

Residence

Address _____ Inside City Limit _____

City_____ County _____ State _____

Date of Birth_____

Place of Birth _____

Education _____Ancestry _____

Married ☐   Single ☐   Widowed ☐   Divorced ☐

If Married: When _____

　　　　　　　Where _____

　　　　　　　Maiden Name of Spouse _____

Father's Full Name _____

Mother's Full Maiden Name_____

Social Security Number _____

　　　　　　　　　　　　　　　　　　　　　　　　Active ☐   Retired ☐

Occupation_____

Employer _____

Previous Employers_____

Resident of _____ Since _____

Prior Residence _____

_____

Military Service _____ War _____

Entered Service

Date _____ Place _____

Service Number _____ Rank _____

Organization _____

Separated from Service

Date _____ Place _____

Please have available a copy of the discharge papers.

Names of Living Children and Town of Residence:

_____

_____

_____

_____

_____

_____

Living Brothers and Sisters and Town of Residence:

_____

_____

_____

_____

_____

_____

How Many Grandchildren: _____Great-grandchildren? _____

Office Held and Lodges & Organizations Belonged to:

_____

_____

_____

_____

_____

Schools Attended, Dates if Graduated

_____

_____

_____

_____

_____

Appendix E
The Widow's Might
Ministry: How It All
Fits Together

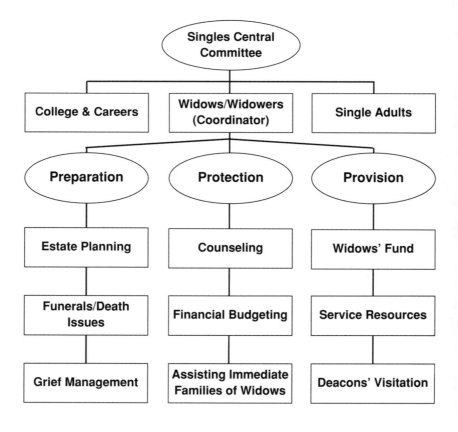

Appendix F
Widows in the Bible

Pentateuch
Gen. 38:11
Gen. 38:14
Gen. 38:19
Exod. 22:22
Exod. 22:24
Lev. 21:14
Lev. 22:13
Num. 30:9
Deut. 10:18
Deut. 14:29
Deut. 16:11
Deut. 16:14
Deut. 24:17
Deut. 24:19
Deut. 25:5
Deut. 25:9
Deut. 26:12
Deut. 26:13
Deut. 27:19

Historical Books
Ruth 4:5
Ruth 4:10
1 Sam. 27:3
1 Sam. 30:5
2 Sam. 2:2
2 Sam. 3:3

2 Sam. 14:5
2 Sam. 20:3
2 Sam. 27:3
2 Sam. 30:5
1 Kings 7:14
1 Kings 11:26
1 Kings 17:9
1 Kings 17:10
1 Kings 17:20

Poetical Books
Job 22:9
Job 24:3
Job 24:21
Job 27:15
Job 29:13
Job 31:16
Job 31:18
Ps. 68:5
Ps. 78:64
Ps. 94:6
Ps. 109:9
Ps. 146:9
Prov. 15:25

Prophetic Books
Isa. 1:17

Isa. 1:23
Isa. 9:17
Isa. 10:2
Isa. 47:8
Isa. 47:9
Isa. 54:4
Jer. 7:6
Jer. 15:8
Jer. 18:21
Jer. 22:3
Jer. 49:11
Lam. 1:1
Lam. 5:3
Ezek. 22:7
Ezek. 22:25
Ezek. 44:22
Zech. 7:10
Mal. 3:5

Gospels
Matt. 22:24
Mark 12:19
Mark 12:21
Mark 12:40
Mark 12:42
Mark 12:43
Luke 2:37
Luke 4:25
Luke 4:26

Luke 7:12
Luke 18:3
Luke 18:5
Luke 20:28
Luke 20:47
Luke 21:2
Luke 21:3

Acts
Acts 6:1
Acts 9:39
Acts 9:41

Epistles
1 Cor. 7:8
1 Tim. 5:3
1 Tim. 5:4
1 Tim. 5:5
1 Tim. 5:6
1 Tim. 5:9
1 Tim. 5:11
1 Tim. 5:14
1 Tim. 5:16
James 1:27

Revelation
Rev. 18:7

125

BIBLIOGRAPHY ❧

Baker, Don. *Pain's Hidden Purpose.* Portland: Multnomah Press, 1984.

Bayly, Joseph. *The Last Thing We Talk About.* Elgin: David C. Cook Publishing Co., 1973.

Brosterman, Robert, and Thomas Brosterman. *The Complete Estate Planning Guide.* New York: McGraw-Hill, Inc., 1964; Mentor Books, 1987.

Burkett, Larry. *The Complete Financial Guide for Single Parents.* Wheaton: Victor Books, 1991.

Caine, Lynn. *Being a Widow.* New York: Arbor House, 1988.

Carter, Malcolm. "Saving Widows from Still More Losses," *Money* (May 1981): 89–94.

Clinebell, Howard. *Basic Types of Pastoral Care and Counseling.* Nashville: Abingdon Press, 1984.

Cornils, Stanley. "Does Your Church Take Care of Its Widows?" *Christianity Today* (July 15, 1983): 60.

————. *The Mourning After.* Saratoga, California: R. & E. Publishers, 1983.

Craige, P. C. *The Book of Deuteronomy.* The New International Commentary on the Old Testament. Grand Rapids: Wm. B. Eerdmans, 1976.

Cushenbery, Donald C., and Rita Crossley Cushenbery. *Coping with Life After Your Mate Dies.* Grand Rapids: Baker Book House, 1991.

D'Arcy, Paula. *When Your Friend Is Grieving.* Wheaton: Harold Shaw Publishers, 1990.

Decker, Beatrice. *After the Flowers Have Gone.* Grand Rapids: Zondervan Publishing House, 1973.

de Vaux, Ronald. *Ancient Israel: Its Life and Institutions.* Translated by John McHugh. New York: McGraw-Hill Book Company, Inc., 1961.

DiGiulio, Robert C. *Beyond Widowhood: From Bereavement to Emergence and Hope.* New York: The Free Press, 1989.

Fairbairn, Patrick. *Pastoral Epistles.* T & T Clark, 1874. Reprint. Minneapolis: James & Klock Publishing Co., 1976.

Featherstone, Robert A. "Widows and Widowers." In *Singles Ministry Handbook,* ed. Douglas L. Fagerstrom. Wheaton: Victor Books, 1988.

Fensham, Charles F. "Widow, Orphan, and the Poor in Ancient Near Eastern Legal and Wisdom Literature." *Journal of Near Eastern Studies* 21 (April 1973): 129–39.

Fisher, Ida, and Byron Lane. *The Widow's Guide to Life.* Englewood Cliffs: Prentice-Hall, Inc., 1981.

Frishkoff, Patricia A. and Bonnie M. Brown. *Preparing . . . Just in Case.* Corvallis: Oregon State University Family Business Program, 1992.

Gallagher, Barry M. *How to Hire a Lawyer.* New York: Dell Publishing Co., 1979.

Gates, Philomene. *Suddenly Alone: A Woman's Guide to Widowhood.* New York: Harper & Row, Publishers, 1990.

Gryczynski, Edward S., Lewis J. Tolleson, and Elizabeth H. Audie. *Help Your Widow While She's Still Your Wife.* Alexandria: The Retired Officers Association, 1988.

House, H. Wayne. "Distinctive Roles for Women in the Second and Third Centuries." *Bibliotheca Sacra* 146 (January 1989): 41–54.

Kent, Homer, Jr. *The Pastoral Epistles: Studies in I and II Timothy and Titus.* Chicago: Moody Press, 1958.

Langer, Marion F. "How to Live As a Widow?" *Pastoral Psychology* 18 (December 1967): 29–32.

Lauderdale, Beverly. "Preparing for Widowhood." *Ministry* (September 1980): 26–28.

Lewis, Alfred Allan, and Barrie Berns. *Three Out of Four Wives: Widowhood in America.* New York: Macmillan Publishers Co., Inc., 1975.

Lightner, Candy, and Nancy Hathaway. *Giving Sorrow Words.* New York: Warner Books, 1990.

Lopata, Helena Znaniecki. *Widowhood in an American City.* Cambridge: Schenkman Publishing Company, Inc., 1973.

Maddison, D. C., and A. Viola. "The Health of Widows in the Year

Following Bereavement." *Journal of Psychosomatic Research* 12 (July 1968): 297–306.

Malatesta, Victor J., Dianne L. Chambless, Martha Pollack, and Alan Cantor. "Widowhood, Sexuality and Aging: A Life Span Analysis." *Journal of Sex and Marital Therapy* 14 (Spring, 1988): 49–62.

Manning, Doug. *Don't Take My Grief Away*. San Francisco: Harper & Row Publishers, 1979.

McGrath, Anne, Maureen Walsh, Nancy Linnon, and Sharon Golden. "Living Alone and Loving It." *U.S. News and World Report* (Aug. 3, 1987): 52–56.

Nye, Miriam Baker. *But I Never Thought He'd Die*. Philadelphia: The Westminster Press, 1978.

Radmacher, Earl D., and Elizabeth Tucker. "Caring for Widows— The Church's Responsibility." *Communicator* (Fall 1987): 2–6.

Rogers, Donald. *Teach Your Wife to Be a Widow*. New York: Henry Holt and Company, 1953.

Sanders, J. Oswald. *The Incomparable Christ*. Chicago: Moody Press, 1952.

Shields, Laurie. *Displaced Homemakers: Organization for a New Life*. New York: McGraw-Hill Book Company, 1981.

Silverman, Phyllis, and Adele Cooperband. "Widow-to-Widow: The Elderly Widow and Mutual Help," *The World of the Older Woman*, vol. III, Frontiers in Aging Series, ed. Gari Lesnoff-Caravaglia. New York: Human Sciences Press, 1984.

Sissom, Ruth M. *Instantly a Widow*. Grand Rapids: Discovery House Publishers, 1990.

Speicher, Terri S. "A Father to the Fatherless." *Focus on the Family* (February 1990): 18–20.

Stahlin, Gustiv, "Χήρα." In *Theological Dictionary of the New Testament*, ed. Gerhard Kittel. Grand Rapids: Wm. B. Eerdmans, 1975: 440–65.

Teterud, Wesley M. "Alone Again." *Moody Magazine* (May 1991).

Whaley, John, and Roger Williamson. *Setting Your House in Order*. Grand Rapids: Resources Development Associates, 1976.

Wiersbe, Warren W., and David W. Wiersbe. *Comforting the Bereaved*. Chicago: Moody Press, 1985.